Shopping & Leisure Guide
Lower Normandy

© 2001 by Passport Guide Publications
19 Morley Crescent, Edgware
Middlesex HA8 8XE

Written By:	Sharron Livingston
Contributor:	Richard Bampfield MW
Published By:	Passport Guide Publications
Enquiries :	Tel: 020 8905 4851
Email:	Sharron@channelhoppers.net
Web site:	www.channelhoppers.net
Advertising Enquiries:	Logie Bradshaw Media Ltd
	Strathallan House, Midland Road
	Hemel Hempstead
	Herts HP2 4LS
	Tel: +44 (0) 1442 233331
	Fax: +44 (0)1442 231131

ISBN: 095243199 8

Contents

Contents

Introduction

Normandy is divided into two administrative regions: Upper Normandy and Lower Normandy.

This raison d'être of this book is to be of service as a guide to Lower Normandy. More specifically, Cherbourg, Caen, Bayeux and Mont St. Michel.

Within this area enjoy the fabulous Calvados coast including the elegant seaside resorts such as Honfleur and the highly fashionable Deauville.

Savour the Norman history through its architecture, numerous sights and museums and enjoy insights into the Norman culture and traditions through its gastronomy. Combine all of this with a good dose of retail therapy. Nothing beats a bargain, and you can come away with Norman cheese, perhaps some Calvados or cider or even bargain wine.

Our researchers have lovingly pinpointed the best restaurants, hotels and shops and also managed to negotiate a some special offers for Channel Hoppers. Enjoy!

Enjoy peace of mind cover at home and abroad

with Green Flag European Services

Did you know that **Green Flag** offers an extensive range of European Services to bring you peace of mind throughout your visit to Europe?

As well as offering an exceptional UK vehicle rescue service to its 4 million members, **Green Flag** offers a comprehensive range of motoring and travel-related European Services to both members and non-members.

The following services are available to non-members:

European Motoring Assistance

Our European Motoring Assistance package brings you complete peace of mind in the event of a breakdown, accident, fire or theft whilst abroad. It includes passenger and vehicle repatriation if needed.

European Travel Insurance

Our policy brings you cover for a variety of situations including injury, cancellation of your holiday, theft of

your property, additional accommodation costs and legal expenses.

Ferry and Eurotunnel Booking Service

Green Flag can help you with your travel plans by booking your channel crossing at a time which fits in with your travel plans. We also offer valuable discounts on selected ferry crossings and our experienced operators can offer helpful advice.

All **Green Flag** European Services offer high standards at great value for money prices. So next time you're planning a visit to Europe, give us a call.

Call European Services FREE
0800 400 638

Green Flag
Motoring Assistance

Hopping Over

Cross-Channel travel remains a popular British pastime. Lower Normandy in particular is becoming a popular short-break destination especially since faster cross-channel vessels have been introduced onto the Portsmouth/Cherbourg route.

Seasoned travellers know that the secret to enjoying a hassle free trip is a little planning. If you need help, turn to a travel club. These exist to find the best cross-Channel deals and package breaks.

Hopping Over

**The perks of shopping abroad start on board
where products are available at
low French duty paid prices.**

From	To	Company	Crossing Time	Frequeny
Poole	Cherbourg	**Brittany Ferries** Tel: 0870 5360 360 Check in: 45 mins www.brittany-ferries.com	4hrs 15mns 6hrs 30mns	2 daily Overnight
Portsmouth	Cherbourg	**P&O Portsmouth** Tel: 0870 2424 999 Fasct craft Check in: 45 mins www.poportsmouth.com	5hrs 8 hrs 2hrs 45mns	2 daily Overnight 2 daily
Portsmouth	Caen	**Brittany Ferries** Tel: 0870 5360 360 Check in: 45 mins www.brittany-ferries.com	6hrs 6hrs 30ms	2 daily Overnight
Portsmouth	Le Havre	**P&O Portsmouth** Tel: 0870 2424 999 Check in: 45 mins www.poportsmouth.com	5hrs 30mins	3 daily

FROM WILLIAM THE CONQUEROR
TO THE BATTLE OF NORMANDY

CAEN

1000 YEARS OF HISTORY

Office de Tourisme
CaEN
OFFICE DE TOURISME
★ ★ ★ ★
Place Saint-Pierre
14000 CAEN - France
Tél. +33 2 31 27 14 14
Fax +33 2 31 27 14 18
E-mail : tourisminfo@ville-caen.fr

**Le Mémorial
de Caen**
UN MUSÉE POUR LA PAIX

BP 6261
14066 CAEN Cedex 4 - France
Tel. +33 2 31 06 06 44
Fax +33 2 31 06 01 66
E-mail : resa@memorial-caen.fr
www.memorial-caen.fr

How Do You Say?

It's amazing how a few choice French phrases will break the ice with the locals and greatly enhance your enjoyment.

Pleasantries

Nice to meet you	Enchanté
Yes/No	Oui/non
Good Morning/Good Day	Bonjour
How are you?	Ça va
Good Evening/ Night/ Bye	Bonsoir/bonne nuit/Au revoir
Excuse me	Excusez-moi
Thank you / You're welcome	Merci / Je vous en prie

Being Understood

I don't speak French	Je ne parle pas français
I don't understand	Je ne comprends pas
Do you speak English?	Parlez-vous anglais?
I don't know how to say it in French	Je ne sais pas le dire en français

Eating Out

A table for two please	Une table pour deux, s'il vous plaît
The menu please	Le menu, s'il vous plaît
Do you have a children's menu?	Avez-vous un menu pour les enfants?
We'll take the set menu, please	Nous prendrons le menu, s'il vous plaît
We would like a dessert	Nous aimerions du dessert
The bill please	L'addition, s'il vous plaît
Is service included?	Le service est compris?
Do you accept credit cards?	Acceptez-vous les cartes de crédit?

Hotels

I'd like a single/double room	Je voudrais une chambre pour une personne/deux personnes
I reserved a room in the name of:	J'ai réservé un chambre au nom de:
I confirmed my booking by phone/letter	J'ai confirmé ma réservation par téléphone/lettre
My key, please	Ma clé, s'il vous plaît
What time is breakfast/dinner?	Le petit déjeuner/Le dîner est à quelle heure?
I shall be leaving tomorrow	Je partirai demain

Paying

How much is it?	Ça coûte combien?
I'd like to pay please	On veut payer, s'il vous plaît
Can I have the bill please?	L'addition, s'il vous plaît
Can I pay by credit card?	Puis-je payer avec une carte de credit?
Do you accept traveller's cheques/ Eurocheques/Sterling?	Acceptez-vous les cheques de voyages/Eurocheques/Sterling?

Cherbourg has the largest artificial harbour in the world spanning over 3000 acres.

The commercial port of Cherbourg sits on the mouth of the windy landscape of the Contentin peninsular. Cherbourg's most outstanding feature is its impressive artificial harbour. It welcomes three seafaring companies ferrying in one and a half million UK citizens into the port annually.

Though Cherbourg is not blessed with interesting architecture or even a good range of museums, this naval seaport does have a certain touristic appeal,

and historically it tells an interesting if short story.

When Louis XVI the Sun King ruled Normandy, he commissioned Vaubhan to design a series of fortifications. Though the projects were realised, they were later abandoned by the King. Napoleon Bonaparte relaunched them and they proved effective in deflecting attack from the British. On **Place Napoleon** close to the port, a statue of Napoleon sitting on a bronze horse, quite aptly shows him pointing at England.

Sadly, life is rife with irony, and these defences proved to be a curse when in 1944 the Germans effectively used the town as their fortress.

The **Fort du Roule**, which perches on a 325 (100m) high mountain, is worth visiting for two reasons. Firstly the view from the top gives an aerial insight into the port's location and an overall panoramic view.

Secondly the ramparts are home to the **Musée de la Guerre et la Libération,** a museum which documents the Allied landing and the liberation of the area.

Alternatively, a subdued pleasure can be enjoyed in the **Parc Emmanuel-Liais**. Green fingered visitors may be a little surprised at the display of rhododendrons and azaleas in full bloom in spring, or the tropical floral formation in the summer.

The town beach also has its appeal, beckoning ramblers onto its soft sands to enjoy a warming walk while a hair tusseling sea breeze provides a natural coolling fan.

Tourist Office
2, quai Alexandre III
50100 Cherbourg
Tel: 00 33 (0) 233 93 52 02
Fax: 00 33 (0) 233 53 66 97

Markets
Cherboug has some appealing markets.

These are held:

Tuesday & Thursday
the rue des halles

Wednesday
Next to St Pierre church

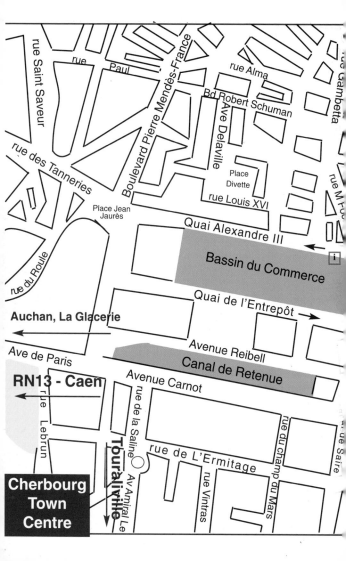

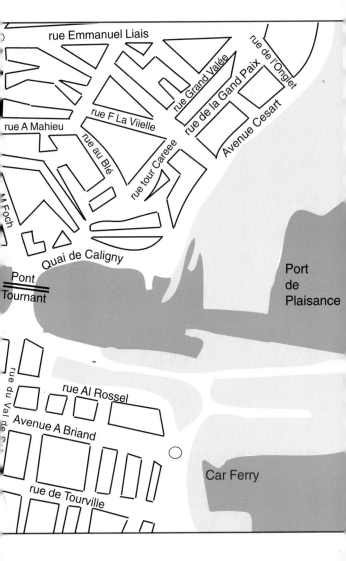

CENTRE E. LECLERC

**509 Rue des Métiers
ZI Sauxmarais
Tourlaville**

**Tel : 00 33 233 236 565
Fax: 00 33 233 220 723**

**Open: Monday to Saturday
from 8.30am to 7.30pm
open: Wednesday
8.30am to 8pm**

**Huge choice of wines, beers,
spirits and alcohol**

also at:
Querqueville-Cherbourg & Caen

 ²⁴/ ₂₄   Eurocard,

What's On Offer at E. Leclerc?

Wine	FF
Muscadet Sèvre et Maine MA Cordelier	9.95
Muscadet Sèvre et Maine MA Caracteres	16.95
Côtes du Rhône Gregoire XI	18.90
Buzet Chantet Blanet	22.50
Côtes de Bourg Chantet Blanet	23.50
Côtes de Bourg Samonac	37.50

Sparkling Wine	FF
François d'Aubigne Brut/Demi Sec	5.80
Muscador Blanc or Rosé	9.40
Paul Bur	16.95
Charles Volner	24.60
Saumur Oxer	24.95
Café de Paris	27.05
Kriter	29.05
Crémant d'Alsace	29.50

Champagne	FF
Pol Carson	86.90
Moët et Chandon	142.05
Veuve Clicquot	149.75

Gin	FF
Gin Edmonson 70cl	43.80
Gibson 70cl	52.70
Gordon Gin 70cl	68.45

Whisky	FF
Four Roses 70cl	62.35
Paddy 70cl	82.10
William Peel 1L	86.65
Long John 1L	90.60
Label 5 1L	94.60
Grants 1L	97.20
Jack Daniels 70cl	109.10
Chivas Regal 70cl	139.25

Beer	FF
Biere Eco (4.5%) 24 x 25cl	28.70
Heineken 12 25cl	34.05
Kanterbrau 24 x 25cl	41.05
33 Export 24 x 25cl	42.30
Stella Artois 24 x 25cl	47.50

How to get to Centre E. Leclerc

From the port follow signs to Caen to the first roundabout. Take the second exit on the right in the direction of Cherbourg. At the next roundabout take the first on the right. At the first traffic lights, turn right where the shop is well in sight.

Cherbourg Sights

Le Musée Thomas Henry
Centre Culturel
rue Vastel

Thomas Henry Fine Arts Museum is regarded as the third most significant museum in Normandy. It was founded in 1835 and now houses 300 permanent exhibits. These include paintings, sculptures, ceramics and crockery dating as far back as 15th century to the 19th century. The works of Guillaume Fouace, Millet and the sculptor Amand are included in the display.

Open throughout the year from 9am to 12 noon and 2pm to 6pm. Closed Mon. Entry fee: FF15

Public Garden
Avenue de Paris

This is a good place to bring the kids. There is a menagerie, a large aviary and a play area. It is open all year round.

Emmanuel-Liais Botanical Park

Access to this lovely garden is at the corner between La rue de l'Abbaye and la rue Emmanuel-Liais.
The botanical collections and tropical greenhouses are open throughout the year except weekends and bank holidays.

Museum of War and Liberation
Roule Mountain

This is a war museum depicting the Allied landing and the liberation. Open every day from 1st May to September 30th From October it is closed on Mondays.

Abbaye Du Vou
Rue de L'Abbaye

This 12th century church was founded by Mathilde, the daughter of King Henry I of England. Entry is free.

Cherbourg Sights

The Trinity Church
Place Napoléon

The church dates from the 14th and 15th centuries. It has a 15th century Baptismal font. The interior and decor of the upper gallery of the nave includes carved panels with 15th century multi-coloured bas-reliefs depicting scenes from the life of Christ and the Dance of Death 'Danse macabre'
Open daily 8.30am to 7pm.

Maritime Museum
Chantereyne
Port des Flamands -
Tourlaville

The museum can be visited from 1st September until the end of June.

Tour of Cherbourg Harbour

Tours starts from the Port Chantereyne and last 1-3 hours. Information is available from the tourist office Tel: 02 33 93 75 27.

How to Get to
The Tourist Office
The Town Centre
The Port de Plaisance

From the port turn right. At the roundabout, with the statue of Minerva, take the 2nd exit: follow the sign to Centre Ville - Town Centre.

The Tourist Office
**2 quai Alexandre III
Tel: 00 33 233 93 75 27**
As you approach the traffic lights make sure you are in the left hand lane then turn left over the swing bridge. Then turn left to **quai Alexandre III**. The tourist office is on the right.

Town Centre
As you approach the traffic lights make sure you are in the right hand lane and go straight on into **rue Marcheval Foch** then first left into **rue de Château.**

Port de Plaisance
As you approach the traffic lights, stay in the right hand lane and turn right into **Quai de Caligny** which turns into **Ave. Cassart** after the **statue of Napoleon**. The facing sea is the Port de Plaisance.

Auchan Hypermarket
RN13
La Glacerie
Tel: 00 33 (0)233 44 43 44

English: No
Tasting: No
Payment:

Parking: Yes
Open: Tues-Sat: 8.30-10pm
Closed: Sun

How To Get There
From the ferry follow the road to the left passing Esso Garage. At roundabout bear right in the direction of Caen. Over 3 roundabouts straight on following Sauxmarais/Caen. Uphill 4kms, turn right at roundabout, double back at next roundabout and turn right

---

The hypermarket phenomenon never took off in the UK, but in France, hypermarkets are everywhere. Carrefour hypermarkets are usually the largest and most modern, followed closely by Auchan. E Leclerc although a tad smaller, tends to offer slightly better value. Although each hypermarket has its own personality, there are similarities. Compared with UK supermarket

Carrefour Hypermarket
quai de l'Entrepôt
51000
Cherbourg
Tel: 00 33 (0)233

English: No
Tasting: No
Payment:

Parking: Yes
Open: Tues-Sat: 8.30-10pm
Closed: Sun

How To Get There
From the ferry follow signs to Centre Ville turning right at the roundabout.Straight over the next roundabout Folow thebend to the left - the port is on the right - turn right onto the bridge. Go round the docking basin to the railway as if you are coming back on yourself. Turn left to Carrefour Hypermarket.

E Leclerc Hypermarket
Rue des Métiers
ZI Sauxmarais
50110 Tourlaville
Tel: 00 33 (0)233 23 65 65

English: No
Tasting: No
Payment: 💳💳

Parking: Yes
Open: Mon-Sat: 8.30-7.30pm
Fri 8.30-8pm
Closed: Sun

prices, the hypermarkets are always a great place to visit to stock up on almost any product. In tems of alcohol it is especially worthwhile to buy the beer and the

How To Get There
From the ferry follow the road to the left passing Esso Garage. At roundabout bear right following signs to Caen. At 2nd roundabout exit on the right, direction Cherbourg, then at the next roundabout take the first on the right. At the first traffic lights, turn right, the shop is ahead.

sprits at hypermarkets, simply because sheer size and buying power ensures that a vast and diverse range is on offer. The beer range includes the increasingly popular Belguim beers alongside their continental range.

Intermarché
Rue de Grand Pré
50110 Tourlaville
Tel: 0033 233886020

English: No
Tasting: No
Payment: 💳💳

Parking: Yes
Open: Tues-Sat: 8.30-10pm
Closed: Sun

How To Get There
From the ferry terminal follow the road to the left. Pass the Esso Garage, over the roundabout following signs to Caen. Left at next roundabout. Follow road for 1km bear right in the Caen direction into Ch de la Marine over crossroads into rue due Grand Pre.

Shopping in Cherbourg

The wine range in all hypermarkets tends to be almost entirely French, perhaps with the odd 'vin etranger' jostling for attention. Probably their best vinous range is the Champagnes and sparkling wines. Other products worth buying are included in the 'Other Shopping Ideas' section. Be sure to look out the 'Promos' for their sales tend to be very generous.

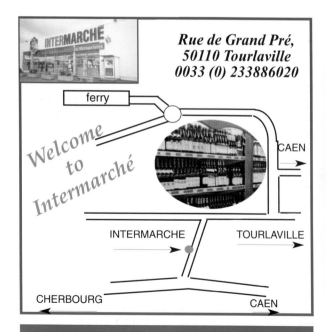

Rue de Grand Pré,
50110 Tourlaville
0033 (0) 233886020

ferry

CAEN

Welcome to Intermarché

INTERMARCHE — TOURLAVILLE

CHERBOURG — CAEN

Shopping in Cherbourg

Intercaves

27 Bis, Ave Aristide Briand
Cherbourg
Tel: 00 33 (0)2334 48 03

English: A little
Tasting: No
Payment:

Parking: On street
Open: Tues-Sat: 9.30-
12.15pm
& 2.30pm -7.15pm
Mon: 2.30pm-7.15pm

This small outlet is located conveniently close to the port and belongs to the Intercaves group. The wines are from around France including some unusual Champagnes.

Bag- in-the-box wines feature too with wine en-vrac starting at FF9.95 per litre.

Ferry Superstore

P&O Ferry Boutique sARL
BP46
50652 Cherbourg Cedex
Tel: 00 33 (0)233 43 27 26

English:	Yes
Tasting:	A Little
Payment:	£, Eurocheques, travellers cheques
	Irish Punt
Parking:	Yes
Open:	8am-8pm Mon to Sat
	8am-noon Sun

Though The Ferry Superstore is a newcomer to Cherbourg, they seem to have embraced the vinous desires of the British taste bud quite well. Their

> **How To Get There**
> From the roundabout at the exit of the ferry terminal turn left following 'fret' sign directly into the car park of the Ferry Superstor.e.

range leans towards the flavoursome fruity wines of the New World, good value French country wines or wines from countries with developing wine industries, such as Chile and Romania. In this way they have managed to keep prices mostly below the £4.99 price point beyond which the British are reluctant to venture.

Shopping in Cherbourg

* Star Buys *

Chardonnay Vin Mousseaux Brut NV FF 22.90
Light, fresh apple aromas, soft flavours and easy drinking.

"Solo" Merlot, Kressmann Vin de Pays d'Oc FF19.90
Ripe plum aromas with a mellow follow through on the palate. Drink this red with food or just enjoy. Great value.

Chardonnay, Banrock Station FF29.90
Lots of sunny tropical fruit aromas, with delicious melon and lychee flavours knitted together with a backbone of crisp acidity. Fabulous.

Minervois "Cuvée la Folly" FF17.90
A red with great depth of colour and flavour offering ripe, juicy fruit and a long tangy finish. It is so easy to drink that at 12.5% abv it may well lead to folly. Best drunk with food.

Mourvedre/Shiraz, Yenda Vineyards 1999 FF24.90
Baked, hot, traditional Oz style red. Sweet fruit with wine gum flavours.

Château Tanesse Bordeaux Blanc Sec FF19.99
A dry white with creamy sherbety aromas, flavoursome and a gripping finish. A good example of what good value Bordeaux blanc can be.

Hardy's Nottage Hill Cabernet Sauvignon/Shiraz FF39.90
Enticing blackcurrant aromas, richly flavoured with lashings of blackcurrant, soft tannins and a good balance of acidity. Terrific value.

Merlot, Concha y Toro FF32.50
A ripe juicy red with soft, fruity flavours and attractive aromas of blackcurrant and green pepper. No sharpness or tanin makes this good value wine very easy to drink.

Normandy Wine Warehouse

71 Ave Carnot
50100 Cherbourg
Tel: 00 33 (0)233 43 39 79
www.normandiewine.com

English:	Yes
Tasting:	A Little
Payment:	£, Eurocheques, travellers cheques
	irish Punt
Parking:	Yes
Open:	10am to 10pm daily

It is very easy to shop at the British owned Normandy Wine Warehouse. Both the proprietor, Chris Bullimore and his team, are bilingual and very friendly The service is attentive and there is a 'try before you buy' policy on selected wines.

The hand-picked range on offer is predominantly French with many good value country wines and wines from lessor known regions in the Rhône, the South and South-West.

How To Get There

From the ferry terminal follow signs to Centre Ville. Turn left at roundabout with statue. Go through 2 sets of lights, take middle lane. Park in their car park just before the Shell garage. If you pass Macdonalds you have gone too far.

Offerings also include a handful of the most popular wines from Italy, South Africa, Australia, Chile, Argentina and Germany. In all, there are around 200 wines. There is also a range of beers, ciders and spirits including the local tipple Calvados.

Shopping in Cherbourg

* Star Buys *

Cuvee Laurent, Vin de pays de L'Aude, Dmn de la Ferrandiere 1999 FF18
Vivid, youthful colour and scented juicy aromas. The warm flavours are typical of southern France, blackcurrant and herbs. Excellent value.

Fleurie, Dmn de la Cour Profond 1999 FF23
A fine example of a Fleurie, purple hue, fully, lightly scented, gamey aromas and a chewy, juicy texture. Excellent.

Merlot, Dmn de la Ferrandiere Vin de Pays d'Oc 1999 FF19
Lots of black fruits and flavour. Very good value.

Château Ballan-Larquette, Bordeaux 1997 FF26
A mix of black berries and tobacco. Excellent value.

Gigondas, Dmn de Montvac, Rhône 1998 FF46
This warm Rhône opens in the glass releasing delicious sweet and savoury flavours. Drink now or enjoy more in 2 years.

Côtes de Montravel, Château de Laulerie 1996 FF36
A great aperitif medium sweet wine and excellent value.

Côtes du Rhône Blanc, Château de Marjolet 1999 FF26
A delightful wine with peach aromas and delicate apricots flavours and scented aftertaste. Good Value.

Saint Veran, Dmn de la Croix Senaillet, Burgundy 1999 FF49
A top class full flavoured, fruit driven white Burgundy. Excellent value.

Vieilli en fûts de chêne, Marquis de Pennautier 1999 FF34
Sweet, juicy oaked aromas with lots of flavour. If you like oaked chardonnay, you'll love this one. Great value.

Muscadet de Sèvre et Maine Sure Lie, Dmn de la Houssais 1999 FF25
A top Muscadet, mineral flavours, fresh, dry and crisp but not tart Great value.

Shopping in Cherbourg

Les Tonnelles Du Val
102 rue Médéric
50110 Toulaville
Tel: 00 33 (0)233 22 44 40

English: Yes
Tasting: A Little
Payment: £, Eurocheques,
travellers cheques

Parking: Yes
Open: 9am-12noon &
2pm-7pm
Closed: Sun

How To Get There
From the ferry terminal head towards the Esso garage and turn left a the roundabout 'la route portuaire'. Follow the road into Aristide Briand, At the end turn left into rue Médéric. After the lights you can drive straight in or park opposite.

Special Offer
5% off
for
Channel Hoppers
just show your guide

Les Tonnelles du Val is a little out of town but well worth the detour to get to this drive-in wine outlet. Maybe it's the layout or maybe it's the atmosphere created by Evelyn and Christian Lethelier, but it is easy to be taken with this little

outlet. Many of the wines are French country wines but there are also wines from all regions many of which are in the affordable £1-£5 price range. There are a number of Bag-in-Box wines which are generally Vin de Pays and some spirits.

28

Shopping in Cherbourg

The Wine & Beer Company

Carrefour Shopping Centre
quai de l'Entrepôt
50100 Cherbourg
Tel: 00 33 (0)233 22 23 22

English:	Yes
Tasting:	A Little
Payment:	£, Eurocheques
	Irish Punt
Parking:	Yes
Open:	8.30am-8.30pm
Closed:	Sun

The Wine & Beer Company, if nothing else is certainly prolific, boasting outlets in the major French channel ports. This outlet is conveniently situated within the Carrefour Hypermarket shopping centre. Pop into the hypermarket for the large range of beers and spirits and other goodies. But for a good value range of wines and Champagnes from around the world, make your way here.

How To Get There

From the ferry terminal follow signs to Centre Ville turn right at the roundabout.Straight over the next roundabout Folow thebend to the left - the port is on the right - turn right onto the bridge. Go round the docking basin to the railway as if you are coming back on yourself. Turn left when you will see Carrefour Hypermarket. The outlet is in this centre.

∗ Star Buys ∗

Cawarra Colombard Chardonnay, Lindemans FF19
Flavoursome, easy drinking dry white. Terrific value.

Konunga Hill Shiraz/Cabernet, Penfolds FF47
A full bodied Oz wine, firm flavours and black fruit with a hint of spice and oak. Great value.

Bayeux

Bayeux :
The 'Cradle of The Norman Empire'

Bayeux is situated on the site of Augustodurum, an old Roman settlement, cradled within a valley formed by the river Aure. The Norwegian Viking King Rollo - later the first Duke of Normandy - took it over in 890. In 905 he became a grandfather when his daughter gave birth to a son. Since then Bayeux has been known as the 'Cradle of the Norman Empire'.

Unlike its neighbouring towns, Bayeux has remained perfectly preserved throughout the D-Day fighting. Dom Aubourg, a chaplain at St-Vigor's Priory cleverly persuaded the Allied troops that the Germans had fled thus averting potentially damaging air raids. As a result the tricolour was raised on 7th June 1944 and Bayeux became the first French city to enjoy liberation. Later that month when Charles de Gaulle visited he was quoted as saying *'I am happy to be back on the soil of France and to find myself in this patriotic Norman town'.* - no doubt a sentiment shared by many French visitors.

Bayeux centre is most famous for its tapestry, its cathedral and more recently, the **Memorial Museum of the Bataille de Normandie** (Blvd Fabian Ware open May-Sept 10-6pm) Here life size models and military hardware help vividly tell the story of the Battle of Normandy. Directly opposite is the **British War Cemetery**, where 6000 British soldiers are buried.

The town itself is an intimate package of cobbled streets and tiny side roads, enveloped by a ring road. The longest street in Bayeux extends from one end of the town to the other, reflecting the town's changing ambiences along its stretch. It starts at **place St-Patrice**, the scene of the Saturday market and ends at with the pedestrianised area at rue **St Jean**. Identified initially with the name **rue Patrice**, it then becomes **rue St Malo**, followed by **rue St Martin**, both busy stretches. It finally becomes **rue St Jean**. Here there are a myriad of restaurants, eateries and souvenir shops. It is also the site for the lively Wednesday market. Through some of its street names Bayeux volunteers echoes of its past street activities. Names such as **rue de la Poissonnerie** - fish market and **rue des Cuisiniers** - cookery road - and **rue Laitière** - milk market street, tell all.

Rue Franche - Free Street, was named by a saint - St-Manvieu who miraculously brought a child back from the brink of death. He decreed that anyone about to die should not use this street.

Rue Franche is also home to some of the best examples of Bayeux's well-preserved 15th-18th century old houses. These old stone and timber framed buildings together the watermills which track the river Aure somehow add an air of prosperity and elegance to the town.

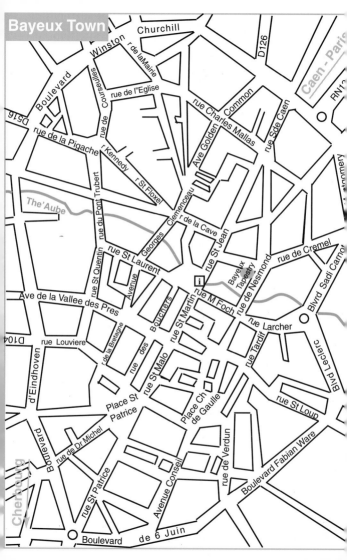

Bayeux Sights

**Centre Guillaume
le Conquérant
rue de Nesmond**
The Bayeux
Tapestry -
Tapisserie de la
Rein Mathilde

A scene of the Bayeux Tapestry commissioned to
celebrate William's victory at Hastings

The 1476 Bayeux
Cathedral inventory
refers to the most
famous tapestry in
the world as :
'*Item, a very long piece of
cloth embroidered with
pictures and inscriptions
representing the conquest of
England*'.
This long piece of cloth
measures 70m by 0.5m
and embroided in muted
reds, greens and blues. It
is a stunning piece of
work, shown over 58
scenic panels. It was
commissioned by William
the Conqueror's half
brother Bishop Odo. The
work was carried out by
nuns in England and
supervised by Queen
Mathilde, to be completed
in time for the opening of
Bayeux Cathedral in
1077. Open daily: 9am-7pm.
Oct-Mar. Closed 12.30-2pm
Admission FF38

**Cathédral Notre Dame
Places des Tribunaux**
A short walk from Centre
Guillame Le Conquérant
is the the former home for
the Bayeux Tapestry - the
Notre Dame Cathedral. Its
depth is an amazing
100m and with the arched
ceilings being 22m high.
The arches are decorated
with Scandinavian and
Anglo-Saxon designs. In
some places there are
monkeys and monsters.

Caen

Caen's history is made of illicit liaisons, forbidden love, religious intrigue & war time devastation.
You couldn't make it up!

It must have been sunny that day in Falaise in 1027. The young Arlette was washing her laundry at the laverie. As usual, she had lifted her skirt, baring her legs, to keep her skirt dry before settling into the task. But on this day the task remained undone. For her beauty attracted more than just the attention of the passing 17 year old Robert the Magnificent, son of Richard II, Duke of Normandy.

The ensuing moment of unbridled passion changed the course of Franco-British history and the face of Caen forever when nine months later, William The Bastard was born.

Caen is pronounced 'Kon' with an almost silent 'n'

William grew up and took his place as the Duke of Normandy. He was later known as William the Conqueror when, during the Norman invasion of 1066, he defeated King Harold at Hastings and became the first Norman King of England.

By 1051, William, while still the Duke of Normandy, had fallen madly in love. She was reluctant at first, declaring she would rather become a nun than marry a bastard, Mathilde the daughter of the Count of Flanders seemed firmly resolute. Undaunted by the rejection, William raced to her father's castle in Lille, he dragged her by her plaits until she eventually fell into his arms; an unusual wooing tactic but it seemed to work.

Unfortunately, Mathilde was William's distant cousin and their marriage caused a religious uproar. Both he and Mathilde were ex-communicated by the Pope who considered marriage between relatives to be most unacceptable. Nevertheless, persuaded by Lafranc of Bec, Pope Nicholas II finally agreed to sanction the marriage in 1059 after each vowed to build an abbey in Caen.

William's abbey is known as the **Abbaye aux Hommes** and a mile away, Mathilde's is called **Abbaye aux Dammes.** As a result, church-state relations improved as did the commercial aspects of Caen. As for the marriage, it lasted for 30 happy years.

William was quick to recognise Caen's strategic potential and shaped the town into the capital city for lower Normandy. The fortification which completely encircled Caen,was completed in 1058. Later William's castle **Château de Caen**, was built in 1060 midway between the two Abbeys. Much of the castle was reduced to rubble in World War II but at the summit of the castle ramparts there is still a chapel, a museum and of course a good view of the city of Caen.

Caen

Successive dukes also took up residence in Caen but unfortunately, during its history Caen suffered a catalogue of disasters.

King John's charter in 1203 saw an increase in trade and prosperity and the English were expelled in 1204.

All was well until 1346 when the English returned. Tempted by rich pickings, Edward III ransacked the town, and then sacked it.

In 1377 the Hundreds Years War between France and England began and was particularly unkind to Caen. It was finally ended by King Charles VII when he reclaimed it in 1450.

Caen was the scene of combat again during the Wars of Religion which ended in 1589. Even more unfortunate was that the damage incurred by the wars was further compounded by plagues of 1584, 1592 and 1631.

Caen is no doubt most remembered as being the prime target in June for the 1944 D-Day landings. The Battle of Caen lasted two months before the Germans were defeated, reeking more and more devastation as each day passed. By August 22nd, though the Battle for Normandy had ended, over 75 per cent of Caen had been destroyed.

It seems poignantly prophetic that the word Caen derives from an old celtic word meaning 'battlefield'.

Caen has had to undergo a lengthy process of

restoration in order to regain its cultural status, especially as Préfecture of Calvados and the capital of Basse (Lower) Normandie. Reconstruction with a eye on modernity, has been successful in giving a pleasant, spacious feel to this bustling City. Even though the City may seem a little functional there are more than 460 hectares of green space to add some natural colour.

In building the character of the city, the restoration initiative also took pains to restore many historic buildings, monuments and architecture. Consequently, every now and then there are pockets of medieval streets mainly around the **Place St-Sauveur** and **Rue Froide.** These are graced with lovely 18th century buildings made from Caen's famous creamy gold limestone.

How to Get to Caen from Ouistreham

The nearest port to Caen is Ouistreham, a fifteen minute drive away.

From the port follow the signs to Caen, passing the Credit Maritime on the right. Stay on the D84 sign-posted Caen.

Normandie Wine Warehouse is on the left. At the roundabout take the second exit.

On the right there is a shopping centre with an Esso Garage. If you are low on petrol, fill up here and get any provisions.

Go over another roundabout and the road becomes D515. Stay on this road for ten minutes until you get to Caen.

***Caen has so many church towers
that it has been dubbed
'The Town of 100 Bells'***

L'Abbaye Aux Hommes rue Guillaume-le-Conquérant

The Abbey For Men was built by William the Conqueror to appease the Pope for marrying his cousin Mathilde. William was originally buried in St. Etienne church, attached to the Abbey. Sadly, the Huguenots ransacked the tomb during the Wars of Religion leaving a single thigh bone. The abbey's 18th century monastic buildings are now home to the town hall whose oak panelled rooms are decorated with 17th, 18th and 19th century paintings. The chapter house is used for marriages and the refectory for receptions.
Daily guided tours of the monastic buildings start at 9.30am, 11am, 2.30pm and 4pm. Admission FF10.

L'Abbaye Aux Dames Place de la Reine Mathilde

Mathilde of Flanders, William's wife, also had to build an abbey to appease the pope. It is located one mile away on the opposite side of town to William's abbey, north east of the centre. The church contained within the abbey - **La Trinité** - is where Mathilde was interred in a simple black marble tomb. It is a fine example of Normandy Romanesque art. Also in the abbey are monastic buildings which overlook the town centre. It has been lovingly restored, adorned with green lawns and is now the seat of the Lower Normandy Regional Council.
Free daily guided tours at 2.30pm & 4.30pm.

Le Château de Caen
Ducal Castle
rue Montoir-
Poissonnerie - entry via
Porte sue la Ville

The castle was once the seat of the Dukes of Normandy. The Kings of England used it as their residence too. It contains Church of Saint-Georges which is now a museum, the Hall of the Exchequer, **Musée des Beaux Arts** Caen's noted fine arts museum and **Musée de Normandie.** The Musée de Normandie has an archeological and ethnological collection in twelve exhibition rooms illustrating man's cultural evolution throughout the history of Normandy. All of Caen can be seen from the castle's towers.

Musée des Beaux Arts
Open 9.30am-6pm

Musée de Normandie
Open 10am-6pm Wed-Fri
Closed 12.30-2pm Sat-Mon
Admission free.

St-Pierre Eglise
rue Montoir-
Poissonnerie

The church has a 72m spire which can be used as a landmark all around the town. Though there has been a church on this site since the 7th century, this one dates back to the 13th century.

Tourist Office
Hôtel d'Escoville
14 place St-Pierre
Caen
Tel: 00 33 231 27 14 14
Closed between 1-2pm.

A beautiful building typical of early Renaissance in Caen.

During the summer there is a currency exchange service here.

Little Tourist Train
Departure Point Place Saint Pierre opposite the Tourist Office. The trains takes you on a journey of of historical discovery. Lasts 45 mins. Cost FF20

The Caen Memorial Esplanade Eisenhower

In 1944, at a mere eighteen years of age, Jean-Mare Girault had joined the emergency squads to get Caen back on its feet. The experience made a lasting and profound impression on the young man. When he later became the mayor in 1983 he persuaded his council colleagues to establish a permanent memorial to the war. By the time the memorial opened its doors in 1988 it had been renamed as 'Museum For Peace', thereby bestowing a more positive image. Both the modern architecture and its setting are fittingly impressive. With each

---

A Tour of The D-Day Beaches by car

Follow 140km stretch of coast starting from the river Orne, at Caen to Les Dunes de Varneville on the Contentin Peninsula. You can stop off and visit the many museums along the way. The beaches on route are often referred to by their war time codes. Amazingly, You can still see small amounts shrapnel on the sands.

*From Caen take the D515 to Ouistreham and follow the signs for the Circuit du Débarquement. Following the D514 you will pass **Sword** and **Juno** Beaches. On the cliffs by the **Gold** beach at St-Côme de Fresne there is information about D-Day landings. The D514 continues to **Omaha** beach where the majority of American troops landed. Further on turn right to Grandcamp-Maisy where there is the Ranger museum. Move onto the N13 in the direction of Cherbourg and exit on the D913 for Ste-Marie-du-Mont. In the village, signs tell of the events of D-Day. The road continues to **Utah Beach**.*

Caen Sights

step you take you become more and more immersed in the history of the last 100 years especially the WWII and in particular the Battle of Normandy and the D-Day landings. The images are poignant and the three twenty minute miniature epic films, shown on extremely wide screens, leave you speechless with emotion. The museum also runs guided tours of the D-Day landing beaches. A combined ticket costing F370 will give you access to the museum and include the beach tour.
Tel: 00 33 231 06 06 44
Open daily 9am-7pm.
Admission FF67. WW2 veterans, free.

La Colline Aux Oiseaux 'Bird Hill'
Ave Amiral-Mountbatten
The 80 acre flower park for peace was opened on the 50th anniversary of the Allied landing. The

Active Leisure
Boat Trips
Trans-Canal
96 quai Vendeuvre
Tel: 00 33 231 34 00 00
Available from March to November. Departs from Caen at 9am, 12.15pm 3.15pm and 7pm. Costs FF77 for adults and FF38 for children. Lasts two and a half hours and passes the Châteaux Beauregard and Bénouville and Pegasus Bridge. You can dine on board and reserve a meal in advance.

flowers are varied and include a rose garden with 670 varieties amongst the 1500 on display. All the gardens are dedicated to peace. You can picnic, there are games for the kids and a panoramic view to enjoy. With all this natural beauty, it is hard to believe that this was once a rubbish tip.
Open daily.

Caen Sights

The walled City of Caen was a firm favourite with William and Mathilde. Even today Caen remains a pleasure to walk through.

A tour around Caen need only be contained between William's and Mathilde's two landmark abbies: the Abbaye-aux Hommes. and Abbaye-aux Dames. This mile long area contains everything of interest that Caen has to offer.

Bassin St Pierre
Pleasure boats and yachts are always moored here.

Place Courtonne
The square offers a car park and a bus junction except on Sundays when there is a busy market. Though it is mainly an antiques market, most other things are sold too.

Tour Guillaume-le-Roy
The tower serves as a good land mark for the traffic that passes all around it. It was once part of the town's ramparts.

Vieux Quartier de Vaugeux
This pedestrianised area is full of cosmopolitan restaurants in timbered buildings. La Bourride, one of Caen's most popular restaurants is located here.

Rue St Pierre
This is a pedestrianised road which houses **Musée de Poste** (Postal Museum) which is a fine example of the 16th century half-timbered buildings often associated with Normandy. Other medieval buildings are inhabited by stylish chocolate shops, patisseries and jewellers.

Caen Insights

Rue Froide

The **Eglise St Saveur** corners with Rue St Pierre and Rue Froide. In fact it was once called Notre-Dame de Froide Rue. There is a plan on the wall in rue Froide showing how the area looked in 1817.

Place St-Saveur

This is a multi purpose square - its a car park and a major open-air market held on Fridays. Around the square are some 18th century mansions and in the square there is a statue of Louis XIV.

Rue Aux Fromages

The look of the area changes here. The roads are cobbled, the buildings half-timbered and there are a number of antique dealers trading here.

Rue Ecuyere

This is another pedestrianised street with mainly antique dealers. Number 42 rue Ecuyere, a 15th century building was once home to a Vicomte de Caen.

Place Fontette

The law courts - **Palais de Justice** - are situated on this square. From the bridge enjoy the view over Abbaye aux Hommes and the town hall.

Markets
Place St-Sauveur
Principal Market
held every Friday.

General Shopping
rue St Pierre
Boulevard du Maréchal Leclerc

Antique Shopping
Rue Ecuyère

Restaurants
Place Courtonne
rue du Vaugueux

Carrefour Hypermarket
CC St-Clair
14200 Herouville St Claire
2miles/3km northeast of
Caen
Tel: 00 33 (0)231 46 55 00

English: A little
Tasting: No
Payment: £,

Parking: Yes
Open: Mon-Sat
          9.am-9pm
Closed: Sun

Carrefour is the biggest hypermarket in the area. It is preceded by a petrol station and surrounded by a mix of quality shops and informal restaurants.

Champion
2 rue Garbsen
Herouville St Claire
Tel: 00 33 (0)231 53 16 60

English: No
Tasting: No
Payment: £,

Parking: Yes
Open: Mon-Sat
          9.am-8pm
Closed: Sun

How To Get There
From the port follow signs to Caen, take the Route de Ouistreham, following the signs to Herouville St Claire and then to Carrefour. It is close to the ferry terminal at Ouistreham and can be reached on foot.

On a smaller scale, Champion supermarket manages a similar look. It also has a petrol station but this one is open 24 hours.

Both offer good value shopping, but of course the former has more space in which to pack in the bargains!

How To Get There
From the port follow signs to Caen. Credit Maritime is on the right. Stay on D84 signposted Caen. At the second roundabout thre is a shopping centre within which Champion is located.

Normandy Wine Warehouse
12 Quai Charcot
&
13 rue l'Yfer 14150
14150 Ouistreham
Tel: 00 33 (0)231 36 05 05

English: Yes
Tasting: Yes
Payment: 💳 💳 £

Parking: On the square
Open: 10am -10pm daily

How To Get There
Exit the Ouistreham Ferry terminal and follow signs to Caen. Pass 3 sets of lights and Normandy Wine Warehouse is on the left.

From Caen follow signs to car ferry. The outlet is 800m after the second roundabout. |

Special offer

FREE

Flavour of Normandy for Channel Hoppers

1 bottle of Château de Brouay Normandy cider

just by showing your copy of The Channel Hoppers Guide.

Normandy Wine Warehouse has certainly got a fabulous location. It is the closest outlet to Ouistreham port and you have to pass it either on your way into Caen or on your way back into Ouistreham.

In-store the layout is well designed for browsing. The staff speak English and moreover are able to impart their knowledge of their wines as required.

For recommendations and tasting notes, turn to Normandy Wine Warehouse's entry on page 27.

Shopping in Caen

Cave Saint Etienne
6 Place Monseigneur des
Hammeaux
1400 Caen
Tel: 00 33 (0)231 38 26 80

English: A Little
Tasting: A Little
Payment:

Parking: On the square
Open: 9.30am-12.45pm 7
            3pm-7.30
            Sat 9.30am to 7.30pm
            Sun 10.30am-12.45pm

These are two small,
but inviting upmarket
wine outlet offering wines
from most French regions
as well as Calavados and
cidres. Les Caves Thorel
also has a wine bar with

Les Caves Thorel
Place Courtonne
1400 Caen
Tel: 00 33 (0)231 86 07 46

English: A Little
Tasting: A Little
Payment: Eurocheques,

Parking: On the street
Open: 7am-8pm daily
            Sunday 8am to 2pm

How To Get There
From the port follow signs
to Caen, take the Route de
Ouistreham, then follow
directions to Hotel de Ville /
Abbaye Aux Hommes.

Special offer
Buy **twelve** bottles of
the same wine and
recieve a **10%**
discount

Just show your guide

lovely stone arches giving
the place a very pleasant
ambience.

How To Get There
From the port follow signs
to Caen, take the Route de
Ouistreham, then George
Clemenceau, left at Abbey
aux Dammes, follow the
road into Place Courtonne.

Special offer

Buy **six** bottles of wine
and recieve a **10%**
discount.

Just show your guide

*T*he beautiful Calvados Coast starts at Honfleur and ends at Cabourg. The stretch, known as Côte Fleurie (Floral Coast), a most justified descriptive name, has become increasingly popular since the Pont de Normandie (the Normandy Bridge) bridged the gap between Upper and Lower Normandy in 1995.

The coast stretching between Trouville and Cabourg has also

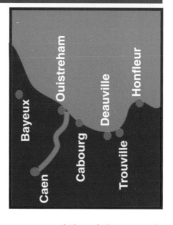

earned the nickname of the 'Norman Riviera', with the pretty, family-friendly Trouville being likened to Nice and the glamourous Deauville

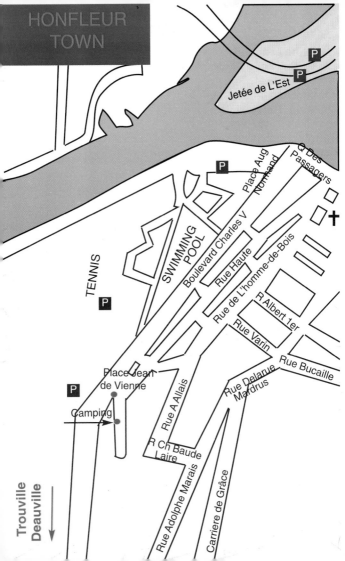

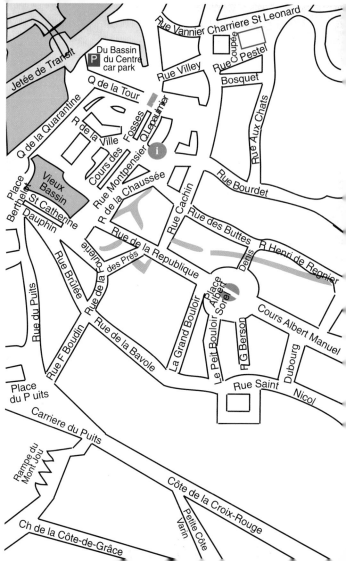

to Cannes.

Honfleur, with its winding alleyways and cobbled walkways simply oozes charm. It is the first port of call from the Seine river and the elegant Pont de Normandy (Normandy bridge) and generally considered the prettiest of any of the towns along the Calvados coast.

For sure, artists seem to think so for they congregate every Saturday in earnest pursuit of capturing some of its charm onto canvass. Their more famous predecessors who have already reaped inspiration from the town include Monet, Sisley, Pissaro, Renoir and Cézanne. They all came here to learn from their mentor Eugène Boudin. You can visit the **Musée Eugène Boudin** and

Musée Eugène Boudin
rue de l'Homme de Bois
Tel: 31 89 45 00

Saint-Catherine Church
Saint Catherine's Square

Musée de la Marine
Quai St-Etienne

Boat Trips
From quai de la Planchette
Tel: 31 89 07 77

From quai des passagers
to Pont de Normandie
Tel 31 89 41 80

From quai de la Quarntine
Tel: 31 89 05 83

Markets
place St Catherine
A Saturday general market

St Leonard
A bio market.

Festivals in Honfleur

June
Seafarers' Pilgrimage

October
Shrimp festival

admire Boudin's work alongside those of Courbet, Monet, and Raoul Dufy.

One of Honfleur's most notable features are the tall, multi-story slate-covered houses. These elegant yet irregular structures are a fine edging for Honfleur's Vieux Bassin, the old port, built by Abraham Duquesne. The ground floor level of the structures houses a myriad of restaurants and bars imbuing the area with lively human activity. Situated at the mouth of the port - the Porte de Caen - there is the imposing 15th century mansion called **the Lieutenance**. This was once the home of the governor of Honfleur.

One block away is the **rue de la Ville.** It was formerly known as The King's Way, and now offers a range of temporary exhibitions housed in former salt warehouses.

An interesting display of history is in the **Maritime Museum**, located in the 14th century St-Etienne church. The subject of the exhibition is Samuel de Champlain who sailed from Honfleur to Canada to found a French colony in Quebec in 1608.

The old town is located on the other side of the harbour. Its busiest area is at place **St Catherine**, where the vibrant Saturday market is held.

The square is also noted for having the largest wooden church in France - **St Catherine's Church**. It was built during the latter years of the 15th

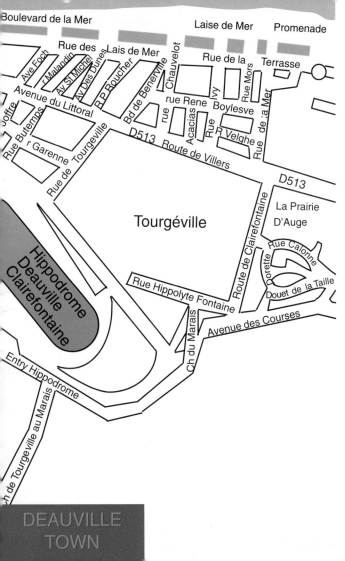

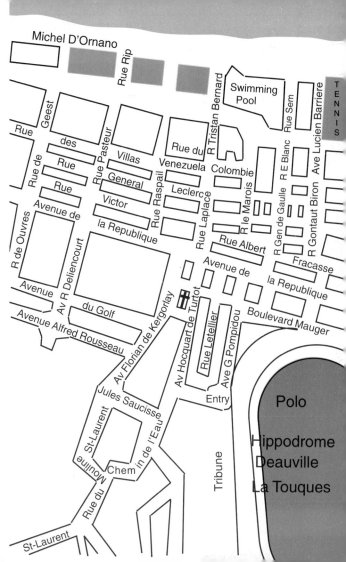

century and the beginning of the 16th century to firstly replace a stone church which had been destroyed during the Hundred Year's War; and secondly to celebrate the departure of the English.

They say a picture paints a thousand words, but an atmospheric panoramic view can leave you speechless. For a fine example, climb the 90m high **Plâteau de Grâce**, to **Mont-Jolie**. It may sound like hard work but you will be rewarded with a fabulous panoramic view of the Seine estuary, the Caux cliffs, the elegant Normandy bridge and of course Honfleur and the Seine Valley.

The next major resorts along the coast are Trouville and Deauville two towns scarcely divided by the tiny Touques river, connected by the Belges bridge; so close, yet so far apart.

Deauville, overtly opulent and terribly expensive, courts the rich, beautiful and the famous. **Trouville**, by contrast, is a modest family town, with its own fishing port, famous boardwalk (planches), and quaint charm. It was made fashionable by Napoleon III in the 1860s when he brought his court to the area. The legacy of these times are the marvellous villas opposite the beach

Deauville, often called the Monte Carlo of the North, is mostly associated with the Jet Set. The 'Deauville season' generally lasts from June to September offering a hefty dose of elitist fun and glamour. During this time the wooden plank promenade, '**Les Planches**' doubles as a fine catwalk for the fashion conscious.

Anyone who has enjoyed the charms of the town owes thanks to the Duc de Morn, Napoleon II's half brother for it was he who recognised that the area was ripe for a racecourse.

By 1864, after four years of development, Deauville was complete. It soon acquired a sense of chic attracting a young Winston Churchill to liberate him from his money at the casino - France's fourth largest gambling venue.

Film stars and an assortment of the rich and famous are attracted here throughout the summer; by the regatta in June, the racing at Clairefontaine Racecourse in July and La Touques and the World polo championships in August.

Deauville is, not surprisingly, known for its stud farms. With over 1400 breeders in Calvados, it is at Deauville that most thoroughbreds are produced.

The opulence and elitism doesn't end there because September heralds the film industry's Festival of American Films. Originally, the festival was held here as a stop gap. Hollywood wanted a prestigious venue for its films, unencumbered by any competition. Deauville fitted the bill and 25 years later, the tradition lives on and Hollywood loves it. Steven Speilberg has been quoted as saying "*In the beginning, we came to see Deauville. Now, we come for the festival, which is well-known on the other side of the Atlantic'* Eddie Murphy calls Deauville "*The most romantic city in the world'*.

The enthusiasm for the festival seems to be spreading. In 1999, the Asian Film Festival was tentatively born in Deauville. This festival is set to become an annual institution acting as a display case for films from Korea, India, Taiwan and Thailand.

The fun continues in October when the Paris to Deauville rally takes place. An elegant procession of famous, beautifully maintained classic cars are on show: Head turning cars such

---

Festivals in Deauville

March
Asian Film Festival

May
Cabriolet and prestige car festival

Hockey Festival

June and July
Jazz Festival

Bridge Tournament

International Horse Jumping show
Club de L'Auto
Tel: 00 33 4 66 23 60 92

July and August
Horse Racing

September
American Film Festival

October
Paris to Deauville Car Rally

Casino de Deauville
Probably the most famous casino in France.
Boulevard Cornuché
Tel 00 33 2 31 14 31 14

Golf
Join the rich and famous at this 27 hole golf course
Tel: 00 33 2 31 14 48 48

as the Bugatti, Delahaye, Talbot, Lagonda, Rolls, and De Soto to name a few, show themselves off to an appreciative public.

Though there are some plush hotels such as the Normandy, the Royal and Hotel du Golf, in the area to cater for the crop of affluent visitors , others such as Yves Saint Laurent and actor Gérard Depardieu own mansions in the area.

As with most French seaside resorts, the night life tends to revolve around the Casino. Deauville's casino offers stylish entertainment and an elegant restaurant and night club.

Cabourg one of the oldest and most architecturally elegant towns in Normandy is shaped by a series of wide avenues linked to geometric semi-circular

Tourist Offices

Honfleur Tourist Office
Place Arthur Boudin
Honfleur
Opposite the Town Hall
Services:
Two hour guided walking tours
Ninety minute boat trips for a better view of the elegant Pont de Normandie.
Tel: 00 33 231 89 23 30

Trouville Tourist Office
32 quai Fernand Moureaux
Trouville
Tel: 00 33 231 14 60 70

Note: Trouville and Deauville share their gare SNCF and gare routière
Tel 00 33 231 88 5 36

Deauville Tourist Office
Place de la Mairie
Deauville
Tel:00 33 2 31 14 40 00
www.deauville.org

Cabourg Tourist Office
Jardin du Casino
Cabourg
Tel: 00 33 231 91 01 09

roads. These stylish street designs alone go a long way towards distinguishing the town. The central hub of the area is endowed with a golf course and a casino. Both venues were much frequented by the famous writer Marcel Proust.

Proust & Cabourg

Cabourg flagrantly flaunts its connections to Proust so blatantly, it seems the town - recognisable as the "Balbec" of Du Côté de Chez Swann - together with the Grand Hotel, located at Promenade Marcel Proust are almost synonymous with the writer.

Proust repeatedly stayed at the Grand Hotel between the years 1881 and 1914, spanning his childhood and adult years. His contrary feelings towards the hotel are were expressed as "*this cruel and sumptuous hotel with its deafening and melancholy tumult*".

Visitors could literally go to town with the Proust theme, starting the day with a madeleine breakfast, taking lunch at its Le Balbec gastronomic restaurant or at its beach-club l'Aquarium and enjoy a green hued cocktail Proust. After a flutter at the nearby casino, a drink can be enjoyed at its bar called Du Côté de Chez Swann.

Visitors, can do as the singer, Sting, did and stay in the very room Proust used for a cost of around FF1200.

In 1907 Proust fell in love with a Monégasque taxi-driver called Alfred Agostinelli. When in the 1980s the Promenade Marcel Proust was inaugurated, the mayor distastefully remarked "*What a shining example Proust sets to the young men of today!*" The comment was a source of much embarrassment for Proust. Nevertheless this love inspired the character Albertine.

The Orne Cultural Tapestry

The Orne country is the epitome of all that is Normandy. The town of Vimoutiers for example, features the **Musée du Camembert**, telling the story of how Marie Harel, credited with developing this famous cheese, in fact was given the recipe from a fugitive priest on the run from revolutionaries.

The nearby Argentan area is known worldwide in equestrian circles for its stud farms, the most famous being Haras du Pin, **the National Stud**. The stud has impressive château and stables edging a horse-shoe shaped courtyard which are collectively known as 'the horses' Versailles'. October and September are full of equine activity especially at the races. These are held at the hippodrome at the nearby village of **Le Pin au Haras**.

The lovely neighbouring countryside of Pays d'Auge is blessed with flowering apple trees and famous for the quality of its Calvados.

The Bocage known as Suisse Normonde contains rivers that trout fishers find ideally suited to their sport, as do canoists and kayak sportsmen. Much of the area's beauty has been left largely untouched by tourism.

It's largest town, Alençon, famous for its lacework, was once the capital of Normandy. After World War II General Leclerc established his headquarters beside the River Sarthe. These days it functions as a Lace Museum as a statue of General Leclerc looks on.

ORNE

For stylish Short Breaks in Normandy

Come and relax with us, Orne is so close to the Ferry ports.

- Land of the horse with the Haras du Pin *National Stud Farm*
- Land of apples Calvados and the birthplace of Camembert cheese
- The ancient tradition of lace making in Alençon and Argentan
- The "September Musical Festival" draws enthusiasts from far and wide
- Relaxing in style in the resort of Bagnoles-de-l'Orne
- Regional products in the excellent hotels and restaurants and typical markets
- Or simple hiking and travelling through deep forests, secluded river valleys
or passing stylish houses and chateaux.

ORNE TOURIST BOARD 88, rue Saint-Blaise - BP 50 - 61002 - ALENCON cedex FRANCE
Tel. +33 2 33 28 88 71 - Fax +33 2 33 29 81 60

- ➤

Please rush me more free information on Orne

Name ....

Address ....

....Tel ....

e-mail ....

I am particularly interested in ....

You can e-mail us at : orne.tourisme@wanadoo.fr

Mont St Michel

The Past

At the dawn of time the rock that is Mont St Michel, was covered over by the sea. Millions of years of erosion sculpted the face of the landscape and the persistent pull of glacial movement eventually separated the rock from the Norman coast providing the islet with quiet isolation. The surrounding quick sands, incredible tides and frequent mists also meant that the rock became almost inaccessible.

The awesome ensuing development of Mont St Michel is literally a dream come true: in 708 St Aubert, Bishop of Avranches had three dreams where the Archangel Michael urged him to build a monastic church on the isolated rocky islet of Monte Tombe. He obliged only after the archangel burnt a hole in the Bishop's skull with his divine finger to prove to him that he was not merely dreaming. By 966, Benedictine monks from St-Wandrille were in residence courtesy of Duke Richard I. By the year 1000 the church was completed.

The site was by now an established pilgrimage destination and attracted many 'miquelots' - archangel Michael followers.

Throughout the ensuing 1000 years, the church has been added to extensively, new buildings have risen and a town grew beneath it. The 11th century saw the founding of the **Romanesque abbey church** over a set of crypts and during the 12th century the **Romanesque monastery buildings** were extended to the west and south.

In the 13th century, when the King of France Philip Augustus conquered Normandy, he wished to promote co-operation. He therefore made a substantial donation to enable the construction of the two storey **Gothic** section to get under way. The architecture of six buildings over three levels is unique in the world and considered to be a masterpiece. It is for this reason that the section is now known as the **"Marvel"** - **"Le Merveille"**.

The 14th century was blighted by the Hundred Years War and so the fortifications were built as an effective protective measure against persistent attacks by the English. In this way Mont St Michel escaped damage throughout the 30 year siege. The English however left behind two 'michelettes' (huge mortars) which still stand at the **Porte de l'Avancée**. This is the only gateway in the ramparts and, to the amazement of visitors, is completely flooded at high tide.

By the 17th century, the living quarters which make up the front of the abbey were finally completed.

During the French Revolution and the Second Empire the abbey was used as a prison and fell into a terrible state of disrepair. In 1863, writers such as Victor Hugo, plunged the plight of Mont St Michel into the awareness and hearts of the public by extolling the spiritual and historical merit of its rehabilitation. It was soon declared an Historic Monument and put into the hands of the Historic Monuments Department in 1874 thereby securing its rightful place within the national heritage.

Since 1966 a small monastic community from Bec-Hellouin has been living there, but access to their quarters is of course barred.

The Future

Over the last hundred years , the Norman coast has been stealthily reclaiming the rock as its own through the gradual process of silting. At the current rate, the rock will have lost its independence In less than a century.

But independence will not be the only loss. The whole appeal, especially to pilgrims, is the image of the rock completely surrounded by water giving an air of mystery which imbues it with an ambience of reflection.

This is why the French government have decided to take action. Currently the rock is connected to the mainland by a notoriously ugly causeway. In high season, there are up to 3,500 cars and coaches parked every day on the mile long strip. It is feared that if governmental inertia prevails, in just twenty years the rock will be surrounded by vegetation and cars. Clearly this is not good for the rock's image.

It is intended that a narrow connecting bridge be built. The car park will be two miles from the rock and access will only be via a mini-bus or by foot. This will ensure that Mont St Michel will be completely surrounded by the sea once again.

A Quick Look UP and Around

Whenever visiting a new place, any tourist feels compelled to look around the shops and make the odd obligatory souvenir purchase. Somehow, this seems incongruous at Mont St Michel. Amazingly the locals do not think so.

It takes some mental acclimatisation to realise that Mont St Michel is not just a spiritual pilgrimage site but also a town making a living through its only two-pronged industry - tourism: selling to and feeding tourists.

Most of this activity takes place in the main road, **La Grande Rue** - a misnomer for this quaint road is in reality a very narrow, winding, rising strip of cobbled streets and steps, filled with souvenir shops, restaurants, cafés and kiosks on either side - a stressful combination for any visitor. Perhaps a preferable way to while away a shopping hour (for that is all you would need) would be at the comparatively spacious abbey-owned shops. These are situated within the 13th-15th century ramparts. Access is via a staircase opposite the post office at the start of La Grand Rue.

Shopping is limited and in any case is not the main event. That accolade remains with the abbey and all roads on the rock lead there, whether you wind your way upwards on La Grande Rue or divert onto the steps that take you through narrow passageways onto the outer ramparts.

As you ascend the ramparts you will get a good view of the bay and the nearby Tombelaine island. Tour leaders like to point out that Tombelaine island is what Mont St Michel looked like when known as Monte Tombe and before the sky scraping churches were built. The highest point - 150m high - is crowned by the gilded statue of the Archangel Michael 150m high topping a 100 year old spire.

The abbey, called 'la Merveille de l'Occident' the Marvel of the West, has the official status of "le Premier Site de France" - the number one tourist site in France. As a national monument, it commands a rather hefty entrance fee especially if you also hire a guiding headset. Nevertheless the visit, when treated as a tour of discovery, is an engaging way to pass a whole afternoon as every nook and cranny has its own story to tell.

Cautionary Note.
Though visually inviting, you are advised not to walk across Mont-St Michel Bay at low tide without a guide. If you wish to, contact:

Maison de la Baie
Genêts
Tel: 33 70 83 42

You can join the mass pilgrimage that crosses in July.

Porte du Roy
(King's Gate)

This is the entrance to the Mount where there are two grand michelettes (mortars) left behind by the English. Moving on over the drawbridge and under the portcullis and through the iron gate leads to the Grande Rue. On the left is Mère Poulard's restaurant famous for its fluffy omelettes.

Mont St Michel - The Museums

The Historical Museum
This museum is divided into six rooms as follows:
Room 1: Fossils from the bay, axe heads and prehistoric tools, paintings and sculptures of the 15th century
Room 2: furniture from the middle ages
Room 3: Sound and light show giving an animated history of the rock. There are 35 wax figures which have been given voices to tell the tale from thousands of years ago beginning with Bishop Aubert's dream in 708 when he was told to build a place of prayer for the archangel of God.
Room 4: A history of the prisons. Apparently up to 600 prisoners were in residence at any one time including some 19th century revolutionaries.
Room 5: The life of the monks within the abbey.
Room 6: A collection of ancient panelling.

The Archeoscope
This is an interesting and dramatic film show narrated by an imposing voice.

You are taken into a cave, an abstract forest with howling winds and water invading everywhere then cataclysms, tidal waves and geological disruption until the Mont Tombe (the rock's former name) is formed. There is also a short opera as the Mont emerges from the depths of the stage and then shown around.

Maritime Museum
There are four rooms.
Room 1: The Captain greets you.
Room 2: Life in the bay
Room 3: The mount is given back to the sea
Room 4: A note about the dangers of wondering around beyond the rock and security.

Mont St Michel

**Top Tips to Make To Ehance
Your Enjoyment On Mont St Michel**

Tip: Prepare mentally for the crush! Mont St Michel is packed with tourists especially in high season - coach loads arrive every day with enthusiastic tourists and school kids who crush into narrow streets.

Tip A good escape from the crowds is to visit the romanesque monastery at the top of the mount during Mass. Sit with the worshippers and listen to the monks as they sing their prayers. This is what the rock is all about.

Tip: It rains a lot! Take an umbrella .

Tip: Take comfy shoes The Mont is very steep. From

bottom to top, there are seemingly infinite steps to climb. Make sure you have comfy shoes on.

Tip: The Mont is not designed for a long break. Two nights is ample.

Tip: Accommodation: Stay on the rock itself. Travel light to avoid having to carry heavy bags to and from your car and then up steep stairs.

Tip: Try an omelette dish at least once. These fluffy ensembles of egg were invented here and are world famous.

Tip: One of the most wondrous moments of the day is watching the tide come in. Don't miss it.

Tip: By nightfall the day-trippers have gone, the rock quietens and the Mont lights up. It is a most beautiful and a romantic time to stroll along the ramparts.

Tip: The view of the Mont is best enjoyed from afar. Seen in silhouette, an image rising through the mist from an undefined base is magical.

Which Wine?

France is one of the leading wine producing countries and this is reflected in the French outlets where most, if not all, of their selection is French. With so much choice, it helps to know a little about French wine.

Firstly, inspect the label for an indication and therefore an assurance of the quality of the wine. The best wines of the regions have Appellation Contrôlées on the label which gives a guarantee of the origin, supervision of production method, variety of grape and quantity produced.

Less controlled but still good value wines, are listed as Vins Délimités de Qualité Supérieure (VDQS) and are worth trying. There are also the Vins de Pays. These are country wines, more widely found in the South of France, which do not specify the exact location of the vineyard but are generally worth a try and often offer the best value for money. Good

examples are Vin de Pays du Gard and the wines from Côtes de Gascogne. Further down the ladder are the Vins de Table. They are varied in quality but are so cheap that they are worth a gamble. You could be surprised for as little at FF5-12.00 (55p-£1.33).

We have very broadly categorised the wine growing areas into seven major regions.
These are: Alsace, Burgundy, Bordeaux, Champagne, Loire, Midi and Rhône.

Which Wine?

Alsace
The Alsace is situated in Eastern France on the German border.

The wine labels from this area differ from the rest of France by calling the wine by the name of the grape rather than the area e.g. Gewürztraminer, Riesling.

If a label reads Alsace AC, this is the standard Alsace wine which is typically Germanic in character, often being aromatic and fruity, but drier than its German equivalent.

A label with Alsace Grand Cru printed on it indicates a higher quality and only the four most highly regarded grape types can be used in its making and they are: Gewürztraminer, Riesling (not to be confused with the German wine of the same name), Tokay Pinot and Muscat. These are medium priced white wines with reliable quality and are generally dry to medium dry. The Alsation wines are great aperitifs and also combine well with fish, poultry, salads or with a summer meal.

Expect to pay: 15-30 francs (£1.66-£3.33) per bottle.

Bordeaux
Bordeaux is in the South West region of France with the Dordogne region on its eastern border and the Atlantic ocean on the west.

The term Claret refers to the red dry wines of this region and wines such as Médoc, St. Emillion and Pomerol which are in the lower price range.

There are also numerous wines known by the name of Château. Quality, especially at the lower end, can be variable. Claret goes well with meat, chicken and cheese.

Expect to pay: From as little as 14 francs (£1.55) per bottle, to more than 100 francs (£12.50) for a top class Château.

Situated between Bordeaux and the Dordogne valley is an area called Bergerac.

Bergerac has a complete range of wines of its own; most commonly Bergerac (red, rosé and dry white), Côtes de Bergerac (red and medium sweet wine), Monbazillac (sweet white) and Pécharmant (fine red).

Expect to pay: 10-16 francs (£1.11-£1.77) for the Bergerac. 30 francs (£3.33) for Monbazillac.

Burgundy
Burgundy is an area of France south-east of Paris running from Chablis at the northern end, down through to Lyon at the southern end. About 75% of the wine production in this region is red with the remainder white.

It is worth noting the area on the label when choosing a Burgundy wine since the more exact the area, the finer the wine is likely to be. The best are labelled 'Grand Cru',followed by 'Premier Cru', 'Villages', a specified region and finally, the most basic will have just Burgundy. The best known of the whites is Chablis which is in the higher price bracket. The Côte de Beaune produces some of the finest such as Meursault and some good light dry wines come from Mâconnais such as Mâcon Blanc and Pouilly Fuissé. All Burgundy white wines are dry and are an ideal accompaniment for fish.

The finest red Burgundy wine comes from the Côtes de Nuits such as Nuits St Georges and the Côtes de Beaune namely Pommard, Volnay and Monthélie.These are best drunk with meat, game and cheese.

Expect to pay: 35-70 francs (£3.88-£7.77) These wines tend to be reliable in this price bracket.

Best known of the reds in the South of this region is

Beaujolais. Beaujolais is divided into the standard Beaujolais AC, Beaujolais Superieur which denotes a slightly higher alcohol content and Beaujolais-Villages which is an appéllation controllée (quality control) given to about 40 villages and considered to be of superior quality

The most prestigious of the Beaujolais wines bear the name of one of the ten communes (Crus). These are worth noting since you will come across them practically everywhere. These are Saint-Amour, Juliénas, Chénas, Moulin-à-Vent, Fleurie, Chiroubles, Morgon, Brouilly, Côte de Brouilly and Régnié (the most recently created, but least distinguished Cru).

These are medium priced red dry fruity wines with the Villages and Communes especially reliable and should be drunk young and served slightly chilled.

Expect to pay: 10-25 francs (£1.11-£2.77) for basic Beaujolais AC. 15-45 francs (£1.87-£5.62) per bottle for Beaujolais- Villages or named Commune.

Midi
(Languedoc Roussillon & Provence)
This region stretches from north east of Marseilles down to the west of Perpignan bordering Spain.

Wines from this region, such as Minervois and Corbières represent good value dry reds. The Vin de Pays (sometimes referred to as Country Wines) of the area offer the best value of all. The label will always show the Vin de Pays description followed by the region.

Expect to pay: 6-20 francs (66p-£2.22) per bottle and a little more if VDQS (Vins Délimités de Qualité Supérieure) is printed on the label.

Which Wine?

Rhône

This area is located south of the Burgundy region and continues due south to the Mediterranean near Marseillesand. The region generally produces robust, full bodied wines.

There is the standard Côtes du Rhône and the Côtes du Rhône Villages which is famous for its dry red wine. If the wine is attributable to a named village (which is shown on the label) the chances are it will be better quality but naturally more expensive. Côtes du Rhône wines accompany cheese and poultry dishes very well.

Expect to pay: 8-20 francs (88p-£2.22) for Côtes du Rhône label wines. 20-30francs (£2.22-£3.33) for Côtes du Rhône Villages.

Loire

The Loire wine region starts at Nantes on the Western Atlantic coast of France and follows the Loire river east to Orléans where it cuts back southeast to Sancerre. The majority of wines produced in this area are white.

The Loire offers the widest variety of wine of any area in France and all have a certain refreshing quality that comes from the northerly position of most of the major Loire vineyards and the character of the soil.

Amongst the many well-known names from this area are Muscadet, Gros Plant Du Nantais, Poully-Fumé and Sancerre being examples of dry whites, and Anjou which is well known for its Rosé.

The Rosé wine is very versatile and can be drunk throughout the course of the meal. The whites are best with fish and salads.

Although named wines are generally a better buy, in our experience it is especially true for Muscadet where we recommend either a named or 'sur lie' over the ordinary Muscadet.

Which Wine?

Expect to pay: 8-15 francs (88p-£1.66) for Gros Plant.
10-22 francs (£1.11-£2.44) for Muscadet.
35-39 francs (£3.88-£4.33) for Sancerre & Pouilly Fumé
10-16 francs (£1.11-£1.77) for Anjou Rosé wines.

If you prefer a medium dry wine then try the Vouvray at 20-25 francs (£2.50-£3.12). Vouvray is also available as a sparkling wine.

Champagne
'I am drinking stars'
Dom Perignon describing his sparkling wine

The most luxurious drink in the world, sparkling wine, suggests celebration - something special. Situated north east of Paris with Reims and Epernay at the heart Champagne is renowned for sparkling wine. The climate, the soil, the art of the wine maker and of course the grapes all combine to make champagne the most celebrated in terms of unmatched quality and reputation. These are usually sold under a brand name e.g. Bollinger, Moët et Chandon, Mumm, Veuve Clicquot etc. which are nearly always dry. If you do not like dry wines, then ask for a demi-sec or even a rosé Champagne. Only wine made in the champagne area is entitled to be called Champagne. Other wines of this type is referred to as 'sparkling' wine. Some have Méthode Traditionnelle on the label which means made in the Champagne method'.

Expect to pay: 56-70 francs (£5.90-£7.77) for lesser known brands.
115 francs (£12.77) upwards for well-known brands.

Champagne comes in the following sizes	
Quart:	20cl
Half-bottle:	37.5cl
Bottle:	75cl
Magnum:	2 bottles
Jeroboam:	4 bottles
Mathusalem:	8 bottles
Salmanazar:	12 bottles
Balthazar:	16 bottles
Nebuchadnezzar:	20 bottles

The Spirits of Normandy

***No vineyards here, but who cares,
in Normandy the apple
is triumphant!***

The apple has its place in all things gastronomic in Normandy and that includes the various liquid nectars that are brought forth by fermented and distilled apple juice: Cider, Calvados and Pommeau.

Cider

A wide variety of apples are grown, and a high proportion are fated to become cider. The different soils from the various apple growing areas, endow their fruit with idiosyncrasies which can be tasted later in an extraordinary variety of ciders.

Good cider (bon bère) is made from apple juice. By law it has to be at least 5% alcohol. The process of secondary fermentation in the bottle results is a naturally sparkling drink (cider bouché) and can cost between FF15-FF100. Like wine it can be medium, dry or sweet but may be very alcoholic and like Champagne it comes with a cork to pop.

Though most cider is factory made, an organisation called Duche de Longueville, close to Dieppe, who are reviving the old-fashioned brew using just one variety of apple. The brand name of this excellent cider is 'Le Duc'.

Most Normans suggest that cider should be drunk with shellfish, chicken, tripe or lamb. It is usually

The Spirits of Normandy

The Cider Trail

If you enjoy cider you may enjoy a drive along The Cider Trail. The route takes you on a round trip, stopping off at the farms that produce the best brew and where you can partake in dégustation (sampling). They are indicated by the 'Cru de Cambremer' signs.

The tour will take around two to three hours.

The route starts in Cambremer, take the D101 in the direction of Rogue-Bainard following the 'Route du Cidre' signs.

The route stops at farms in the following places:

1. Cambremer
2. Grandouet
3. St-Ouen-Le-Pin
4. Bonnebosq
5. Léaupartie

At Léaupartie turn left on to the D85 back to Cambremer.

served in pottery jugs.

Calvados

Calvados brandy is made from small, rosey, flavoursome cider apples. This golden cider-based nectar can be traced back to the 16th century, when Gilles de Gouberville, a French farmer, referred to it as *'eau-de-vie de cider'* in his diary. Three centuries later, apple brandies made in Normandy acquired the name of Calvados. In fact, to merit the name Calvados, the spirit can only be produced in Normandy itself. In any case no other area would be able to produce anything as good. Normandy has been blessed with a fertile land upon which apples have been growing for thousands of years, endowing the farmers

The Spirits of Normandy

with a whole treasure chest of apple varieties. The best example is produced in the Auge Valley where the Calvados produced is distinct for two reasons: Firstly, it is the only Calvados with its own AOC - Appellation d'Origine Contrôlée - a system of quality control; and secondly it is the only Calvados that has to undergo a double distillation process. All other AOC Calvados comes from a number of carefully delimited areas within Normandy where only single distillation is required.

Calvados, sometimes affectionately referred to as 'Calva', is distilled from cider, aged and then finally blended. All Calvados is aged in oak for a minimum of two years and some aged for much longer, endowing

So How Old Is It?

*** or 3 apples
This indicates that the Calvados has matured for at least 2 years in wood

Vieux or Réserve
A minimum of 3 years ageing.

Extra or **XO, Napoléon, Hors d'Age** or **Age Inconnu**
A minimum of 6 years' ageing. In the case of a blended Calvados, only the age of the youngest Calvados is indicated.

Indication of Age
Where the label states an age the spirits contained will be of that age or older.

Vintage
If a vintage is shown, it means the spirits has been distilled in that year.

Appelation Réglementée
Single malted Calvados

the spirit with more subtlety and finesse as the flavours develop and soften. After 15 years of aging it takes on a smooth, dry persona with a scent of ripe apples.

When young, Calvados is fiery and should be approached with some caution. Newcomers should try it for taste first by dipping a sugar lump into the calvados. No need for embarrassment, the Normans do this too.

The labels, are by law, very informative so you can choose between a warming glass of apple brandy or a more elegant older spirit, perhaps to add to a collection. Unless you go for a VSOP or an XO example, Calvados tends to be relatively inexpensive. Expect to pay around FF90 in France (UK price averages £15).

Pommeau

This alcoholic drink is not particularly well-known outside France where it is drunk as an aperitif. Pommeau is a blend of freshly pressed cider apple juice and Calvados and aged in wooden barrels. It is very easy to drink - perhaps too easy and makes a good companion for oysters or foie gras.

Bénédictine

Though not made from apples, this sweet liqueur is a thoroughly French drink indigenous to Fécamp in Upper Normandy. It was originally made by a monk in 1510, and 3 centuries later was resurrected by a successful wine and drinks merchant. He named the drink Bénédictine in memory of its monastic origins. It is made from a variety of

The Spirits of Normandy

aromatic herbs which grow locally on the cliffs. The drink contains 27 herbs but the exact recipe is a well guarded secret. The letters D.O.M which appear on the label stand for Deo Optimo Maximo - which means 'to God the best and the greatest'.

Pear Cider or Perry

This sparkling drink, known as poiré, is made from fermented pears. It is most popular in the wooded area North of Domfront in the Orne but not particularly well-known outside of France.

Shop for your tipple

Cidrerie Viard
Géron nr Bayeux
Tel: 00 33 321 92 09 15

Henri Vaucrecy
31 rue de l'Eglise
Rots, nr Caen
Tel: 00 33 321 26 50 51

Les Caves Thorel
32 rue Neuve-Saint-Jean, nr Caen
Tel: 00 33 321 26 50 51

La Cave de Deauville
48 rue Mirabeau
Deauville
Tel: 00 33 231 87 35 36

Bernard Lebey
Ferme de la Croix, Solier
Tourgéville nr Deauville
Tel: 00 33 231 88 14 10

Au P'tit Pointu
22 rue des Bains
Trouville-su-Mer
Tel: 00 33 321 98 36 20

La Gribouville
rue de l'Homme-de Boise, Honfleur
Tel: 00 33 231 89 29 54

Eau, What A Choice!

It's the best thirst quenching drink there is. It's not alcohol but it's a bargain !

Mineral water, (eau minérale) both still (plate) and sparkling (gazeuse) is exceptionally good value for money and much cheaper to buy in France. Why this is so is perplexing as unlike alcohol, there is no tax to blame.

There is often a vast selection of different brands at the hyper-markets. Some, such as Evian, Volvic and the comparatively expensive Perrier will be familiar, yet some of the lesser known brands are just as good.

In our blind tasting, we sampled a some mineral waters at fridge temperature. Here are a selection of commonly available mineral waters:

Badoit: Slightly sparkling from the Loire.
Ave Price: FF3.50 (35p) 1L
Comment: Slightly salty
Contrexéville: From Vosges. Reputedly good for the kidneys. Has a slightly diuretic effect.
Ave Price: FF2.9 (29p) 1.5L
Comment: Slightly salty.
Evian: From the town of Evian at Lake Geneva.It has a slightly diuretic effect.
Ave Price: FF4.20 (42p) 2L
Comment: Tasteless but thirst quenching.
Perrier: A very well-marketed mineral water from Nîmes. Full of sparkle and is generally used as soda water in France.
Ave Price: FF4.5 (45p) 1L
Comment: Most refreshing with almost no flavour.
River: Sparkling water
Ave Price: FF1.75 (18p) 1.5L
Comment: Slightly chalky on the palate.
Vichy: A sparkler from Vichy.
Ave Price: FF3 (30p) 1.5L
Comment: Like bicarbonate of soda.
Vittel: A still yet rugged mineral water - from Nancy.
Ave Price: FF2.80 (28p) 1.5L
Comment: Refreshing and slightly sweet.
Volvic: A still water from Auvergne filtered through volcanic rock.
Ave Price: FF3 (30p) 1.5L
Comment: Smooth silky taste.

Tobacco Prices Up In Smoke!

With an average saving of £1.80 on a packet of cigarettes, topping up in France makes good financial sense.

Product	France	U.K.
Cigarettes	Av. £	Av. £
Benson & Hedges	£1.99	£4.22
Camel	£2.21	£4.25
Dunhill	£2.62	£4.39
Gauloises	£2.37	£3.75
Gitanes	£1.68	£4.22
John Player Special	£1.74	£3.75
Lambert & Butler	£2.15	£3.75
Marlboro	£2.25	£4.22
Philip Morris	£2.22	£3.85
Rothmans	£2.07	£4.22
Silk Cut	£2.25	£4.22
Superkings	£2.15	£3.97
Tobacco		
Drum 50g	£2.56	£7.00
Golden Virginia 40g	£2.00	£7.47
Old Holborn 40g	£2.25	£7.47
Samson 50g	£2.25	£7.37
Cigars x 5		
King Edward Imperial	£4.00	£8.90
Villager Export	£3.75	£4.60

It is interesting to note that a 20-cigarettes-a-day smoker would have to spend in the region of £1503 in the UK. In France the same would cost just £730. You can in theory buy unlimited amounts of tobacco for personal use both on board the ferries or in France but the 'advisory guideline' is 800. In France, tobacco can be purchased from outlets called Tabacs. These shops are similar to newsagents. Cigarette and tobacco prices are state regulated in France when sold through a tabac. This is not true of tobacco sold in cafés, bars and petrol stations where prices tend to be higher.

Unlike the UK, French supermarkets do not sell tobacco at all.

Most tabacs are closed on Sundays and bank holidays. Most accept sterling and credit cards.

The Epicurean's Tour of The Shops

When shopping in any French town what stands out is the variety of traditional gastronomic shops, some of which have no comparable counterpart in the UK. It must be a cultural thing but very simply, the French like to specialise.

Take the Boucherie for example - the butcher. The Boucherie sells all types of meat and poultry - except pork. To buy pork you need to visit the Charcuterie - which means cooked meat.

The Charcuterie, originally a pork butcher, has evolved into a pork based delicatessen. Visiting a Charcuterie for the first time will shift your perception of the humble pig 'le cochon' in gastronomic terms forever! Now you will see it as pâté, terrin, rillets, rillons, hams, dried sausages, fresh sausages, pieds de porc, andouillettes boudins noirs et blancs. This pork lovers haven also offers ready made pork meals with a selection of plats de jour that just need heating up when you get home.

Horse meat is also popular in France and this is sold in outlets known as Boucherie Chevaline - horse meat butcher, generally identifiable by a horse's head sign.

Cheese, a much revered commodity in France, is produced with exacting procedures by the highly skilled maître fromager (master cheese specialist). The shop to visit to really get the feel of the cheese culture at its best is the Fromagerie - a specialist cheese shop which will probably have around 300 varieties on sale.

A cross between a grocery store and delicatessen is the Epicerie. The store sells cheese and fresh meat amongst other food products. These days the Epicerie is based a little on the Supermarché and an Alimentation Général - a general store - and has lost its authenticity somewhat.

The Epicurean's Tour of The Shops

Normandy offers a wide range of fresh seafood. You can buy the catch of the day from the Poissonerie. This could be a fishmonger or just a stall.

Another example of specialisation in action is the Boulangerie - the bakery. The shelves are stacked with all types of unusual bread and buns and occasionally cakes and quiches too.

But for a fiendishly good selection of cakes and biscuits, it is over to the Pâtisserie for specialist cake, flans and tarts. The Pâtisserie sometimes sells icecream and chocolates too.

Sweets, not the commercial pre-wrapped type, but handmade sweets such as bon-bons, nougat and crystallised fruit, have their own home in a Confiserie or Chocolaterie - a high class sweet or chocolate shop. The products are a little pricey but good quality, delicious and beautifully packaged for you.

For fresh fruit, flowers and vegetables and a myriad of fresh French delights the best place is the Marché - outdoor market. These are generally open on a Saturday or Wednesday.

You could of course, by-pass the specialist shops which offer pleasant insightful echoes of French daily life and culture - a shopping experience unlike any you can have in the UK. You could, instead shop in one of the immense Hypermarché - hypermarkets. The total anonymity that comes with being one of hundreds of trolley pushers walking around thousands of kilometres of floor space in a state of suspended reality is an experience all of its own!

Say Cheese

Take a glass of your favourite wine, break off a little baguette, fill it with your favourite cheese - Voila! a slice of French culture.

The inherent passion for wine within the French culture is closely followed by their love for cheese, so much so that France has become renowned for its remarkably large array of cheeses. Incredibly, the number of different varieties is believed to be in excess of 700. Not only do supermarkets dedicate large areas of floor space to their cheese counters, but the French also have specialist cheese shops.

These quaint shops are called 'Fromageries' (cheese shops) offering cheese in all its colours and consistencies.

Though nasal passages have to grapple with the pungent aroma that hangs heavily in the air, the palate can look forward to a delightful epicurean experience. It is at the fromagerie that the finest cheeses can be found, thanks to the resident maître fromager (master cheese specialist). His highly skilled job combines the complexities of cheese selection, storage and the delicate process of '**affinage**'. This is the art of ageing a young cheese to maturity so that it is offered in its prime. This is especially important as some cheeses are seasonal and when out of season they are in fact out of date. A true cheese buff will know the right time of the year to buy them.

To the uninitiated though, the cheese counter must look like a daunting display of yellow and white hues with the odd shout of blue. No matter how tempting these colours look, one wonders about the taste. Fortunately, it is customary for supermarkets and fromageries to routinely offer **dégustation** (sampling) upon request.

Although not possible to list all cheeses, some may already be familiar such as the famous Camembert - and no wonder as there are over 2000 varieties.

Camembert is a soft cheese with a rind made up of moulds. The best has to be from Normandy from where Camembert originates and more specifically from the area between the rivers Touques and Dives. Though the cheese was first made in 1791 by a local farm woman, the circular wooden box it now comes in was created by a Monsieur Ridel in 1905 so that the cheese could be exported. It was awarded an AOC in 985. Look for the letters V.C.N (Véritable Camembert de Normandie)

for a farmhouse variety.

Fromages fermiers (farmhouse cheese) are considered to be the finest of all cheeses. These are made by small producers using milk from their own farm animals. When unpasteurised milk is used this is denoted with the words 'lait cru'. Other varieties to try are:

Bondard. Soft log shaped double-cream cheese with a fruity taste. The rind is a tan colour. Made from cows milk on farms. It is best in October/ November.

Bondon de Neufchâtel. Made primarily by farms and factories. It is salty to taste with a smooth texture.

La Bouille. Hard, fruity drum shaped cheese made with double cream. Made in small dairies. Best in June and February.

Trappiste de Bricque-bec. Disc shaped mild cheese

made by monks. It has an off-white rind.

Brillat-Savarin. This comes from Forges-les-Eux, north of the Seine. Its triple cream gives this cheese a 75% fat content. It is a soft and mild flat disc shaped cheese with a downy white rind. Factory made. It is in the group of cream cheeses under the Neufchâtel banner after the town of the same name. Records show that cheese was being made in the region of Neufchâtel since 1035. They are easy to spot in their varying heart, disc or obelisk shapes.

Le Brin. A small hexagon shaped cheese. Made from cows' milk, it is mild and creamy. The edible rind has a delicate, pleasant aroma. The special method of production leaves the cheese high in calcium and phosphorus.

Cantorel Roquefort. A speciality of South-West France, this blue cheese is ripened in the caves of Cambalou for at least 90 days in accordance with its Appellation d'Origine Contrôlée. Made entirely from sheep's milk, its distinctive taste is best enjoyed with Barsac or Sauternes wines.

Livarot. This cheese was first made in the Vallée d'Auge in the small town of Livarot. It probably dates back to around1690. It was granted an AOC in 1975. It is aged in airtight cellars lined with hay which probably contribute to its spicy, pungent aroma. It is characterised by its reddish-brown crust and a distinctive flavour.The term Colonel, refers to any of the five variations of Livarot.

Pont l'Evêque. It has had a long history having been around since the 13th century. At that time it was produced by monks under the name of Angelot and in 1720 it won more acclaim

Say Cheese

The Cheese Route

Dégustation - sampling - is the French way. Head for **Lisieux** picking up the signposts on the D4 where it meets with the D579. The route takes you through **Pays d'Auge**, **Camembert** and **Vimoutiers** where you can taste the camembert cheese and the Livarot family of cheeses. Visit the **Musée du Camembert (10 av. du Général de Gaulle tel: 00 33 233 39 330 29)** in Camembert village and learn about Marie Harel who originated this famous cheese. A statue of her stands proudly in the village.

further afield. It was was granted an AOC in 1976. It is square-shaped, small, soft, warm and tender with a gold rind. It is clean and pleasant, even fruity, on the palate. Best in summer, autumn and winter.

Pavé 'Auge. This is the term for the square cheese of lower Normandy. Pont L'Evêque featured above, is one of these.

Rambol. Decorated with walnuts it looks like a small gateau. It is smooth with a mellow flavour.

Société Roquefort. Roquefort has been dubbed 'The King of Cheeses. Made

Serving suggestions:

- Cheese is at its best served at room temperature. Remove from the fridge at least one hour before required.

- Allow 2oz per person for a cheese board and 4oz per person for a cheese and wine evening.

- Select 3-4 different types of cheese for an attractive display, especially on a cheese board.

exclusively from ewe's milk, it is creamy in texture and distinguished by its marbled green and ivory colouring. It has a mild piquant flavour.

Say Cheese

Storage Tips:

Most hard cheeses are freezable as long as they are not overmature when frozen. This is not recommended for soft cheeses. Generally, the following guidelines for fridge storage apply:

- Fresh Cheese (soft cheese) Eat within a few days.
- Blue Cheese Can be kept up to 3 weeks.
- Goats', Ewe's Milk Cheese Will keep for up to two weeks.
- Always store cheese in the lowest part of the fridge wrapped in foil or in an air proof container to prevent drying out.

You can buy your cheese at the hypermarket or alternatively at the fromagerie. Most outlets are happy for you to taste before you buy. Try:

Le Bajocasse
Nonant
nr Bayeux
Tel: 00 33 321 92 09 15

Crémerie du 6 Juin
6 avenue du 6 Juin
Caen
Tel: 00 33 321 85 45 03

Aux Fromages de France
116 rue Saint-Jean
Caen
Tel: 00 33 321 86 14 53

La Ferme Normande
Place du Marché
Deauville
Opposite the market
Tel: 00 33 231 88 17 86

French Bread

It's the law. Every French village must have its own boulangerie (bakery) supplying the villagers with freshly baked bread every day of the week.

Governed by French law, the boulangerie usually emerges as the single most important shop in any village, faithfully providing the villagers with an essential part of their staple diet - bread.

As with all things French an etiquette has evolved around bread. It is generally considered unacceptable to serve bread purchased in the morning in the evening. No self respecting Frenchman would dare to insult his guests in this way. However, left over bread may be used perhaps for dunking into hot chocolate - in specially formulated wide cups - or alternatively can be cooked in soup.

The most famous and popular French bread (both within and outside France) is the long, thin baguette or French stick. It is uniform in length; and its weight - governed by French law - must be 250 grams!

Although the baguette is made simply from soft flour, yeast, water and a pinch or two of salt, it has an appealing fluffy texture and can be enjoyed just as well on its own as it can with food. However, its short life span means that it must be consumed soon after it has been baked. Bakeries routinely bake bread twice a day to ensure fresh bread for a very discriminating public.

Other extreme variations on the baguette are the ficelle (a word which literally means string). It is the thinnest loaf available. In contrast un pain or Pariesenis double the size of a baguette. A compromise is reached with petit pains and the bâtons which are much shorter than the baguette and similar to large rolls.

French Bread

For breakfast (le petit déjeuner) the French will also enjoy a Continental breakfast (better known in France as viennoisie). This includes such delicious treats as the famous pastry style croissant. This familiar crescent shaped roll was Marie Antoinett's inadvertent contribution to the Western breakfast culture. She introduced them to the Parisian Royals in the late 18th century where they proved to be an epicurean hit. In Marie Antoinette's home country of Vienna, however, the croissant had been making a regular appearance at the breakfast table as early as 1683. It was in this year that the Polish, army saved the city from Turkish hands and in celebration the Viennese baked a crescent shaped creation based on the Ottoman flag - voila, the croissant was born!

The croissant is similar to puff pastry - made with yeast, dough and butter. It is usually accompanied by confit (crystallized fruit) or confiture (various flavours of jam). Sometimes it is served with jam, cheese or chocolate and can be savoured hot or cold.

Traditionally, the croissant is dunked by the French into their coffee in specially made wide cups designed for this purpose. This French idiosyncrasy can also be traced back to the late 17th century. The defeated Turks had left some sacks of coffee beans before they left Vienna. These were discovered by a group of Armenian Jews who started the croissant dunking tradition.

There are also many other tempting and unusual styles of bread available at the specialist boulangerie (bakery) or the boulangerie counter at the hypermarket. Here are some suggestions to try:

French Bread

Pain au chocolat. A croissant style bun imbued with chocolate (delicious when warm).

Brioche. A breakfast bun made from yeast, dough, eggs and butter, giving it a wonderful sweet, buttery aroma and taste.

Couronnes. A baguette style bread in the shape of a ring.

Pain aux noix. An outstanding bread baked with walnuts on the inside and on the crust.

Pain aux olives. Bread with olives and olive oil.

Pain brié. Found mainly in Honfleur, a local heavy white bread especially suited to be eaten with shrimps.

Pain de seigle. Made with rye and wheat.

Pain noir. Wholemeal bread.

Pain de son. Wholemeal bread fortified with bran.

Pain de mie. Sliced bread with a soft crust. Used for sandwiches.

Pain biologique. This bread is baked with organic wholemeal flour.

Pain campagne. Flatter than baguettes but also heavier. They have the advantage of staying fresh for longer.

Pain au Levain/Pain à l'ancienne. Both these names refer to French bread made from sour dough. This is one of the oldest styles of French bread there is.

Buy bread at any Boulangerie, especially:

Breant Daniel
126 rue Saint-Pierre
Caen
Tel: 00 33 231 50 22 55

La Paneterie
Rue de la République
Honfleur
Tel: 00 33 213 89 18 70

Specialities at the Pâtisserie

In
true
French
style, even the last course of a meal is not the least. Dinner in any French home will always conclude with a sweet, which if not home made, will be bought from the Pâtisserie - a specialist cake shop. The Pâtisserie may also have a selection of handmade confectionery.

Like French wines and cheese, different areas of France have their own regional indulgences on offer and Normandy is no exception.

Normandy, famous for its apple orchards offers, perhaps unsurprisingly, a large range of apple pies.

"An Apple A Day.... '
.....The Norman Way

Offerings include:

Tarte Normande
An apple pie.

Tarte aux Pommes
Another type of apple pie - which is not so much a pie, more a tart with its pastry base topped with apple slices. It makes its appearance in a variety of shapes and sizes.

Gratin de Pommes Vallée D'Auge
This is no ordinary apple crumble; it is soaked in Calvados (an apple brandy produced in Normandy) and then baked in crème fraîche.

Bourdelots - stuffed, baked apple dumplings

Specialities at the Pâtisserie

Chaussons aux Pommes
An apple turnover.

Gâteau de Trouville
A cake filled with cream
and apples.

Bourdelots
This is translated as
apple dumpling. It is
pastry stuffed, with a
baked apple.

Rabote
Baked apple in pastry.

Douillon
A pastry stuffed with a
whole baked pear.

Soufflé Normande
A souflé flavoured with
apples and Calvados.

Sucre de Pommes
Apple sugar sticks.

Mirlitons
Small tarts containing an
almond and cream filling.

Where to buy pastries

Dupont
73 avenue de la Mer
Cabourg
Tel: 00 33 231 24 60 32

Roland
rue St Pierre
Caen
Salon de Thé attached.
Tel: 00 33 321 86 24 53

Jacques Guesdon
Boulangerie du Parc
14 rue Emmanuel-Liais
Cherbourg
Tel: 00 33 321 53 58 91

Salon de Thé Yvard
5 place de la Fontaine
Cherbourg
Patisserie and tea room
Tel: 00 33 321 53 04 14

Aux Délices de l'Etoile
35 rue Désire le Hoc
Deauville
Tel: 00 33 231 88 22 5

La Petite Chine
Corner of rue du Dauphin &
rue de la Foulerie, Honfleur
Tea room attached.
Tel: 00 33 321 89 36 52

Foie Gras

The Egyptians enjoyed it over 2000 years. Soon the ancient Greeks and Roman Emperors enjoyed it. The French perfected it into an art form during the last 200 years and now you can enjoy it too.

Foie Gras, pronounced *fwah gra*, is a much revered goose liver pate. It literally means *fat liver*. In winter, the geese are force-fed with corn and grain so that their livers became supple and enlarged to produce large quantities of *foie* - liver.

Foie Gras is sometimes augmented with truffles but either way it is available cooked or semi-cooked in tins or jars. The latter condition gives it a longer shelf life in the refrigerator.

Serve it thoroughly chilled but slice it with a warmed knife. Accompany it with toast or baguette and enjoy a truly gastronomic taste of France.

Where to buy Foie Gras

Les Fermiers du Bec
6 Promenade Mme de Sévigné, Caen
Tel: 00 33 2 31 70 25 73

Lejetté
9 rue Grande Rue
Cherbourg
Tel: 00 33 2 33 53 01 37

Le Périgord
29 rue Breney
Place du Marché
Deauville
Tel: 00 33 2 31 811 888

Jean Ouaknine
Haras de la Griserie
Genneville
nr Honfleur
Tel: 00 33 2 31 98 74 52

Sauternes wine is a divine accompaniment with Foie Gras

Other Shopping Ideas

What to Buy At the Hypermarkets

Olives
In general olives (both black and green) are about 30% cheaper in the French supermarkets.

Olive Oil
The finest French olive oils - like French wines - come from named origins and even *Appellations Controllées* - quality controlled areas similar to those of wine. They have a gentle flavour tempered with slight sweetness and are great as condiments, but not suitable for cooking.

These olive oils have low acidity (sometimes as little as 0.2%) which is significant because acidity affects the rate at which the oil deteriorates. Labels of assured finest quality to look out for are 'Huile de Provence' and 'Huile d'Olives Nyons' (the latter is subject to quality control with its own Appellation d'Origine. This sort of quality is expensive and could be up to £30.00 in the UK (less in France). Generally, you are likely to purchase brands that are commercially blended.

Look for either Extra Virgin (Vierge) or First Cold Pressing (Premier Presson Froid) whose acidity is never more than 1%, but is better still at 0.5%, Fine Virgin olive oil at 1.5% or less, and Ordinary Virgin olive oil whose acidity level is 3%. This sort of quality olive oil in the UK is rarely below £6.00 per litre yet in France the price is around FF28.00 (£3.50).

Anchovies
You get a wider selection of anchovies, and at half price in France- good value at the hypermarkets.

Fish
If you have enjoyed a fish or seafood meal, you may be inclined to buy your own to take home. The hypermarkets generally have comprehensive fish and seafood sections or better still, you can visit a fish monger *(poissonnerie)*.

Mustard (Moutard)

Mustard is substantially cheaper in France, and there is a wider selection. Dijon mustard prices start at FF1.75 (22p) for 370g jar of Dijon mustard compared to a typical UK price of 59p for 250g. English mustard is slightly hotter t. Try 'seeded' Dijon mustard; it has a particularly delicate flavour.

Filtered Coffee

This is available widely and at half the UK prices. Try the taste of even the cheapest brands of filtered coffee and you will not be disappointed. A 1kg (4 x 250g pack) can be found for as little as FF29. Try Arabica.

Soft Drinks

Fruit juice, colas and especially bottled mineral water tend to be at least 15% cheaper in France. Water especially is particularly good value sometimes up to 50% cheaper.

Pots & Pans

Le Creuset and Tefal are generally half price in France.

Though shopping at the hypermarkets can be intoxicating, the following shops are specialists and worth visiting:

Glassware

Atelier Beautile
Ferme des Chartrains
Cabourg, Take D279
Tel: 02 31 64 27 15
A workshop producing unique decorated glass..

Martial Mayel
27 rue du Puits
Honfleur
02 31 89 05 06

Stone & Marble
A speciality of Bayeux

SARL La Laiterie
Barbeville, nr Bayeux
Tel: 02 31 21 55 67

Pascal Goujon
les Feugrais
Nonant, nr Bayeux
Tel: 02 31 21 17 33

Other Shopping Ideas

Pottery
A speciality of Bayeux

Poterie Dubost
Noyon-la-Poterie
nr Bayeux
Tel: 02 31 92 56 15

Atelier Ceramique Turgis
Noyon-la-Poterie
nr Bayeux
Tel: 02 31 92 57 03

Atelier du Chuquet
Le Molay-Littry, nr Bayeux
Tel: 02 31 22 18 76

Hervé Coffignal
2 rue du Calvaire
Trévières, nr Bayeux
Tel: 02 31 22 56 73

Tuilerie Normande
Bavent nr Caen
Tel: 02 31 78 80 10

The Garden
In general garden furniture is around 15% cheaper in France. Probably the best place to buy it is at the hypermarket or try:

Truffaut
Route de Paris, Deauville
Tel:02 31 88 18 42
From seeds to tractors

Quality take home meals

Breton Traiteur
1 place de Morney
Deauville
Tel: 02 31 88 22 90
&
148 Boulevard F-Moreaux,
Trouville
Tel: 02 31 88 03 65

Farm Produce

Les Producteurs Augerons
79 rue Louvel et Brière
Touques nr Trouville sur Mer
Tel: 02 31 98 06 60

Fruit & Jam
Buy Bon Maman in the hypmermarkets

Alleaume Fruits
84 rue Saint-clair
La Rivière-Saint-Saveur
nr Honfluer
Tel: 02 31 89 04 48

Other Shopping Ideas

Bruno Fremont
Roncheville
Bavent, nr Caen
Tel: 02 31 78 84 22

Tripe-a speciality of Caen
Daniel Marie
Boucher-Charcutier
30-32 avenue de
Calvados, Caen
Tel: 02 31 94 44 55
Bernard Noël
Charcutier
119 rue Saint-Jean, Caen
Tel: 02 31 86 21 60

L'Amaglio
Charcutier
23 place du Commerce
Grace de Dieu, Caen
Tel: 02 31 52 13 80

R Le Fourkié
Charcutier-Traiteur
42 rue Chapron,
Mondeville, Caen
Tel: 02 31 52 13 80

Chocolate
Les Marianik's
35 rue du Dauphin
Honfleur
Tel: 02 31 89 98 00

100F buys you a
chocolate carving of the
old dock.

Dupont
73 avenue de e Mer
Cabourg
Tel: 02 31 24 60 32

Témoins
69 rue Saint-Pierre
Caen
Tel: 02 31 86 31 88

Hotot
13 rue st-Pierre
Caen
Tel: 02 31 86 31 90

Jeff de Bruges
41 rue Saint-Pierre
Passage du Moulin Saint-
Pierre
Caen
Tel: 02 31 85 51 45

B Paillaud
43 bis rue Maréchal-Foch
Cherbourg
Tel: 02 33 43 04 76

Other Shopping Ideas

TIP:
Serious bargain hunters should time their trip to France with the French sales. These happen twice a year - in January and in August and generally last between one to two months. You can pick up some fantastic bargains!

TIP:
Take a cooler bag with you just in case you want to buy fresh products such as cheese or fish to maintain freshnes and avoid any pungent smells on the journey home.

TIP:
Shops close at lunch time.

Do you know
something we don't?

Tell us about it and you
could get a free copy
The Channel Hopper's
Guide

Othcr Types of Shops on the High Street.

Alimentation Général:
General Store

Pharmacie:
Chemist that sells primarily medicines

Droguerie:
Related to the hardware store, selling primarily toiletries.

Nettoyage à sec:
Dry cleaners

Carrelages
Sells tiles

Tabac:
Tobacconist, the only shop that sells cigarettes and tobacco. Also sells stamps.

Maison de la Presse
Sells magazines and newspapers

Librarie:
Book shop

Quincaillerie:
Hardware store

Take a herd of saucy Norman cows, an apple and pear orchard, and the fruits of the sea and voila! Norman Gastronomy

Norman cooking is most distinctive and not advisable for the calorie conscious. Often double or even triple cream is used to enrich sauces imbuing the food with that unmistakable taste of Normandy.

Norman cuisine is a challenge for the body and what's more the French eat a lot of it. Around 400 years ago a custom began to aid digestion. Unlike the Romans who practiced bulimia, the Normans preferred to aid digestion by creating a little hole 'trou' in the stomach by drinking a glass of Calvados in between the first and second course. If you are on a gourmet

'The Norman Hole' a 400 year old custom of preparing the stomach for a big meal - wash down the first course with a glass of Calvados

adventure, try it and enjoy.

The cow and its many ensuing dairy products together with the apple, cider and calvados appear in most recipes. The most popular sauce is the thick yellow **Sauce Normande**, a whisked mixture of cream and butter added to a cider sauce. It is used routinely to cover practically everything from fish to vegetables.

Apart from yielding its fruit, the sea tends to flood the pastures of Normandy leaving behind its salt on the grass. This greatly influences the flavour of the grazing lambs. The resulting dish is known as **Angeau Pré-Salé,** ready salted lamb!

**Everything stops
for lunch in France.
Take time out to enjoy a pastime the
French take very seriously -
eating!**

You know lunchtime has arrived in France when you see the sign **'fermé'** (closed) on shop doors. As the shops and factories close, the restaurants open for business, offering a choice of cuisine and ambience.

French culinary diversity is very much inspired by France's variety of landscape and locally farmed produce and Normandy is no exception.

Generally three distinct styles of cuisine are evident:

Haute Cuisine
The hallmarks of Haute Cuisine is its rich food and elaborate presentation. This style can be tracked back to Louis XIV's 12 hour feasts in the palace of Versailles.

Cuisine Bourgeoise Cuisine
This style is related to Haute Cuisine. Less elaborate perhaps and best described as high quality home cooking. Well known dishes in this category would be 'coq au vin' and 'boeuf à la bourguignonne', perhaps the French version of 'meat and two veg'!

Nouvelle Cuisine
This trendy cooking style originated in the 1970's. The dishes are generally less rich, fresh ingredients are used and vegetables are el dente - almost raw to optimise their natural flavours and aromas.

Choosing a restaurant is easy as they generally display their menus outside. Steer clear of empty restaurants - in our experience, if a restaurant remains unpopulated by 12.30pm, they generally deserve to be so!

If you have booked a table be sure to be on time, as your table is unlikely to be saved for more than ten minutes. This is especially true on Sundays. The French have a sense of specialness about Sundays. Though lunch is the main meal of any day, on this day, lunch is a gastronomic occasion when everyone likes to eat out 'en famille'. These meals tend to last the around 3 hours. It is worth noting that in most French restaurants, the cheapest set menu meal is not available on Sundays.

Most restaurants cater for the tourists by offering a 'menu touristique' usually written in English or with an English translation, alongside the regional dishes. This is usually good value for money and comprises such dishes as steak and French fries, or perhaps an omelette or simple fish dish; these dishes tend to be associated with the British.

Everything has its time and place and that includes lunchtime.
In France lunch is strictly between **12pm - 3pm**

Not all prices will be highlighted on the menu. The letters SG may sit alongside some dishes and stand for selon grosseur (according to weight). This applies to dishes that, for practical purposes, are sold by weight, such as lobster or fish. In this instance it is advisable to find out the price before you order.

One item that will be missing from any French menu is the traditional two-slices-of-bread British sandwich. You may find the word 'sandwich' referred to on the menu at cafés or brasseries, but it will never be served in sliced bread. The most popular 'sandwich' is the **croque monsieur** which is basically ham and cheese in a toasted **ficelle** (a slimmer version of a baguette). The feminine version of this - **croque-madame** which comes garnished with a fried egg.

Alternatively, you could choose the Prix Fixe menu, a set price menu which may include the plat du jour (dish of the day) or spécialité de la maison (house special). These are a better choice for those wishing to try a local dish, usually seafood or frogs legs - 'cuisses de grenouilles'. Indulge in the à la carte menu or the menu gastronomique for finer quality food.

If the words service compris (service included) or service et taxes compris (service & taxes included) are on the menu, that means the prices include a service charge. However, odd coins are usually left for the waiter. Otherwise, a 10% tip is customary.

Meals are never rushed in restaurants even if you only want a snack and a drink at one of the cafés. You can wile away the time at your leisure but if your are eating to a deadline, pay for your meal when it arrives, as catching the waiter's eye later may prove a challenge.

Restaurant Etiquette

Tip:
To get the attention of the waiter lift your index finger and call **Monsieur** - **NOT** garçon. Calling a waiter garçon will be regarded as an insult and a sure way of of receiving bad service.

A waitress should be addressed as **Madam** or if she is very young, **Madmoiselle**.

Alternatively just say **'s'il vous plaît'**.

Tip:
Do not ask for a 'doggy-bag'. This concept simply does not exist in France.

Tip:
Go for French food while in France. This not only adds to the French experience, but also makes good economic sense; traditional British food and drink such as tea, Scotch whisky and gin or a plate of bacon and eggs are expensive. So check out the menu or 'tarif des consommations' (if in a café or bar) for something that tickles your palate and accompany it with wine (vin ordinaire) or draught beer (pression).

Alternatively French spirits and soft drinks are generally an inexpensive relative to their British counterparts on the menu.

Tip:
When ordering coffee, be specific and say exactly what you would like. Unlike British restaurants, just ordering a coffee will not do because the French have a different idea of how a standard coffee

should be served. They will routinely serve it strong and black, espresso style. The exception to this is during the breakfast meal when coffee is served in large wide-mouthed coffee cups - specially designed for dunking - and milk is a standard accompaniment.

Coffee Styles

Un café, s'il vous plaît
You will receive an espresso coffee, strong and black in a small espresso cup

Un café au lait, s'il vous plaît
You will receive an espresso coffee with milk on the side.

Une crème s'il vous plaît
You will receive a small white coffee

Une crème grande s'il vous plaît
You will receive a white coffee served in a normal sized coffee cup.

Terms on a French Menu

Les Viandes	Meat
L'agneau	Lamb
Assiette Anglaise	Plate of cold meat
Bifteck	Steak
Bifteck haché	Hamburger
Boeuf	Beef
Contrefilet	Sirloin
Entrecôte	Steak
Foie	Liver
Foie gras	Goose liver
Faux filet	Sirloin Steak
Jambon	Ham
Langue	Tongue
Porc	Pork
Rognons	Kidneys
Saucisse	Sausage

Les Poissons	Fish
Anchois	Anchovy
Anguille	Eel
L'Assiette de fruits de mer	Sea food platter
L'Assiette Nordique	Smoked fish platter
Crevette grise	Shrimp
Crevette rose	Prawn
Crustacés	Shellfish
Escargots	Snails
Fruits de mer	Seafood
Gamba	Large prawn
Homard	Lobster
Huître	Oyster
Limand	Lemon sole
Saumon	Salmon
Thon	Tuna
Truite	Trout
Truite arc en ciel	Rainbow trout

Volaille	Poultry
Canard	Duck
Dindon	Turkey
Oie	Goose
Faisan	Pheasant
Perdreau	Partridge
Pigeon	Pigeon
Poulet	Chicken(roast)
Poularde	Chicken (boiled)
Poussin	Spring chicken

Sauce	Sauce
Béarnaise	Sauce from egg yolks, shallots, wine & tarragon
Béchamel	White sauce with herbs
Beurre blanc	Loire sauce with butter, wine &shallots
Beurre noir	Blackened butter
Meunière	Butter & lemon sauce

Divers	Miscellaneous
Braisé	Braised
Brochette	Skewer
Brouillade	Stew with oil
Brouillé	Scrambled
Cuit au four	Baked
Fumé	Smoked
Gratinée	Grill browned
Grillé	Grilled
Poivre	Pepper
Rôti	Roast
Sel	Salt
Suprème	Chicken breast or game bird
Terrine	Coarse paté

Confused?
Some items on a menu look very similar but are in fact very different. Take in this list of to avoid inadvertantly ordering something unappealing.

aiguillette	thin slice of meat
anguillette	tiny eel
brochet	pike
brochette	skewered food
cervelas	a type of sausage
cervelle	brain
gras	fat
gras double	tripe
ris	sweetbreads
riz	rice
sauce tartare	mayonnaise sauce
steak tartare	raw steak

Norman Specialities

Ficelle normande
Ham and cheese pancake or mushrooms in a creamy sauce.

Filet mignon de porc normande
Pork tenderloin-cooked ith apples and onions in cider, served with caramilzed apple rings.

Jambon au cidre
Ham baked in cider.

Marmite dieppoise
Mixed fish soup with white wine, leeks and cream.

Moules à la normande
Mussels in a white wine and cream sauce.

Omelette normande
Omelette with mushrooms, cream, Calvados and shrimps or perhaps apples.

Poulet/veau Vallee d'Auge
Chicken/veal cooked in cider and Calvados with cream and apples.

Salade cauchoise or normande
Potatoes, celery and ham in a cream dressing.

Sole Normonde
Dover sole in cider and cream served with shrimps.

Tord-goule or tergoile
Speciality of Houlgate. A rice pudding flavoured with cinammon and baked for hours.

Tripes à la de Caen
Tripe cooked slowly on skewers.

Are you a vegetarian? Unfortunately, Normandy does not cater well for vegetarians. Crêperies may be a solutio. These establishments are numerous throughout Normandy.

A useful phrase to say to a sympathetic Norman waiter:

Je suis végétarien(ne) il y a quelques plats sans viande?

I am a vegetarian. Are there any non-meat dishes?

Enjoyed a good restaurant?

Don't keep it to yourself. Let us know and you could win a copy of a Channel Hoppers Guide.

sharron@ channelhoppers.net

Specialities of Bayeux

Cider and goat's cheese are tops here. Amazingly in mid-December and July there are entire markets just for foie gras

Restaurants of Bayeux

L'Amaryllis
32 rue St Patrice
Bayeux
Tel: 00 33 231 22 47 94
Tariff: From FF70
Cuisine: Traditional

L'Amirauté
14 rue St Jean, Bayeux
Tel: 00 33 231 21 31 80
Tariff: From FF58
Cuisine: Great sandwiches

Le Petit Normand
35 rue Larcher, Bayeux
16th century house by the cathedral.
Tel: 00 33 23151 85 40
Tariff: From FF95
Cuisine: Traditional, serving local cider.
Closed Sept-June, Sun pm

Le Printanier
2 rue Bouchers
Bayeux
Tel: 00 33 231 92 03 01
Tariff: From FF70
Cuisine: Bistro, service
from lunchtime to 9pm
Closed Sun & Mon am.

La Rapière
53 rue St Jean
Bayeux
Tel: 00 33 231 92 94 79
Tariff: From FF79
Cuisine: Traditional, with
grills, oysters and skate.
Located in Hotel de
Croissant - a side street.
Closed mid-Dec-Jan,
Tues pm & Wed.

La Table du Terroir
42 rue St Jean
Bayeux
Tel: 00 33 231 92 05 53
Tariff: From FF55
Cuisine: As this is
attached to a butcher's
shop owned by Louis
Bisson, the food tends to
be a carnivours delight.
It is famed locally for
charcuteries, terrines,
sausages and meat
based dishes.

La Table du Terroir

Restaurant du Boucher

de la boucherie à la table

Louis Bisson

42, rue Saint-Jean
14400 Bayeux
Tél./Fax 02 31 92 05 53

Restaurants of Cabourg

Le Beau Site
30 avenue Foch, Cabourg
Overlooks the beach
Tel: 00 33 231 24 42 85
Tariff: From FF150
Cuisine: Seafood
Closed: Mon nights, Tues
and Dec & Jan

L'Embarcadere
33 ave de la Mer,Cabourg
Tel: 00 33 231 24 08 33
Tariff: From FF79
Cuisine: Seafood, great
desserts & 17 varieties of
tea. Non-stop service.

Le Royal
37 ave. de la Mer, Cabourg
Tel: 00 33 231 91 81 39
Tariff: From FF99
Cuisine: Fish & crepes
Closed: Tues,18 Jan-12 Feb

Restaurant de l'Hippodrome
Ave Michel d'Ornano
Cabourg
Panoramic views
Tel: 00 33 231 91 81 39
Tariff: From FF215
Cuisine: Fish & foie gras
Open: evenings

Specialities of Caen

Try the **Tripe à la mode
de Caen.**

Chocolate caramels -
chiques - and boiled
sweets - **berlingots** - are
particularly nice.

Caen is also known for its
raspberries available in
season (June, July,
September-October)

Restaurants of Caen
Central Caen offers two
eating areas: **quartier
Vaugeux** where the
restaurants are fairly
cosmopolitan. For more
traditional French cuisine,
head for the streets off
rue de Geôle.

L'Alcide
1 place Courtonne
Caen
Tel: 00 33 23144 18 06
Tariff: From FF78
Cuisine: Bistro serving
traditional French dishes.
Closed: Sat

l'Ambroisie
11 rue des Croisiers
Caen
Tel: 00 33 231 50 30 32
Tariff: From FF75
Cuisine: Mainly fish
Closed: Sat lunch & Sun

Le Boeuf Ferré
10 rue des Croisiers
Caen
Tel: 00 33 231 85 36 40
Tariff: From FF99
Cuisine: Mainly fish, lively
atmosphere.
Closed: Sat lunch & Sun

La Bourride
51 rue du Vaugueux,Caen
Tel: 00 33 231 93 50 76
Tariff: From FF196
Cuisine: Top class intimate
restaurant with a variety of
luxurious food.
Closed: Sun evening, Mon

Le Carlotta
16 quai Vendeuvre, Caen
Tel: 00 33 231 86 68 99
Tariff: From FF92
Cuisine: Brasserie style -
excellent food.
Closed: Aug

Le Dauphin
29 rue Gémare
Caen
Tel: 00 33 23186 22 26
Tariff: From FF95
Cuisine: Norman food but
with variation. Rustic
decor. Situated near the
castle and abbeys.
Closed: Sat lunch, Jul-Aug

Dollys
16-18 Avenue de la
Libération, Caen
Tel: 00 33 23194 03 29
Tariff: From FF30
Cuisine: An English
owned restaurant serving
English food with full
English breakfast,
scones, fish and chips or
just a cup of tea. The
decor is pretty and
pleasant - this is not a
greasy spoon - and the
ambience is friendly and
agreeable. The resturant
is near the Château.
Closed: Monday. Open 9.30
to 7.30pm and food is
served all day

Le Gastronome
43 rue St-Sauveur, Caen
Tel: 00 33 231 86 57 75
Tariff: Approx. FF120
Cuisine: Norman cooking
Closed: Sat am, Sun pm &
1-14 Aug.

Restaurant Kouba
6 rue du Vaugueux
Caen
Tel: 00 33 231 93 68 47
Tariff: From FF95
Cuisine: African, couscous.
Camel murals decor.

La Maison Italie
10 rue Hamon,Caen
Tel: 00 33 231 86 38 02
Tariff: From FF60
Cuisine: Pizzeria, open
every night.

Maître Corbeau
94 rue du Geôle, Caen
Tel: 00 33 231 86 33 97
Tariff: From FF88
Cuisine: Fondue. Even the
decor is full of cheese
iconography.
Closed: Sat am, Sun

La Neustrie
2 Place de la République
Caen
Tel: 00 33 231 8 33 07
Tariff: From FF40
Cuisine: On offer is a
selection of 21 different
types of pizzas. A variety
of fish dishes and grills
are also served.

Le Panier à Salades
24 rue Pierre Girard
Caen
Tel: 00 33 231 34 22 22
Tariff: From FF40
Cuisine: A variety of
salads with or without
meat.

La Petite Marmite
43 rue des Jacobins
Caen
Tel: 00 33 231 86 15 29
Tariff: From FF95
Cuisine: Seafood. Good
service, good food and so
the restaurant is very
popular. Booking in
advance is highly
recommended.

Pomme et Sarrasin
36 rue des Jacobins
Caen
Tel: 00 33 231 50 07 36
Tariff: Various
Cuisine: A selection of pancakes, crepes. They also have a childrens' menu.
Closed: Mon nights. Sun Kitchen open to 9.30pm

Le Pressoir
3 avenue Henri-Chéron
Caen
Tel: 00 33 231 73 32 71
Tariff: From FF75
Cuisine: Unpretentious with local dishes: boudin noir and seafood. There is an ancient cider press, and an olde-worlde look.
Closed: Aug, Sun eve, Mon

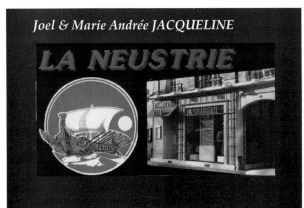

La Poterne
Le Vaugueux
20 rue Porte au Berger
Caen
Tel: 00 33 231 93 57 46
Tariff: From FF98
Cuisine: A variety of dishes are served. There are three types of entertainment on offer: a restaurant, a pub and a night club all in a very pretty house. Soft music, fireplace & warm atmosphere.
Closed: Mon
Open: 6pm-2.30am, kitchen open to 1.30am

La Ferme Saint Hubert
3 rue de la Mer
14800 Colleville Montgomery
14880 Hermanville-sur-Mer
Tel: 00 33 231 96 35 41
Tariff: From FF85
Cuisine: Norman food
This restaurant is situated 2km from the car ferry between Ouistreham &

Hermanville and near the landing beaches - Sword Beach, where the French Commando Kieffer landed on 6th June 1944.

Tongasoa
7 rue du Vaugueux
Caen
Tel: 00 33 231 43 87 15
Tariff: From FF55
Cuisine: From Réunion
Madagascar, Seychelles.
Cocktails served.
Closed: Sun lunch

Le Zodiac
15 quai Eugène-Meslin
Caen
Tel: 00 33 231 84 46 31
Tariff: From FF62
Cuisine: Good for carnivours as the dishes are mainly wood fired grills. Weekly horoscopes greet you at the door and the decor has a Zodiac theme.
Open: Lunch, all day Thurs, Fri. and Sat nights to 10pm

Restaurants of Cherbourg
For seafood head, for the glass fronted restaurants on the **quai de Caligny** where you could enjoy a seaview. For a wider choice, head for the pedestrianized old town.

Au Provencal
27/29 rue Tour Carrée
Cherbourg
Tel: 00 33 233 53 38 24
Tariff: From FF55
Cuisine: Pizza, pasta. The cappuccino is great.
Open: Daily except Saturday lunchtime

Café de Paris
40 quai de Caligny
Cherbourg
Tel: 00 33 233 43 12 36
Tariff: From FF85
Cuisine: Seafood

Café Pompon
1 rue de Maréchal-Foch
Cherbourg
Tel: 00 33 233 53 08 75
Tariff: Various
Cuisine:Creperie/tearoom

La Cale
2 place de la République
Cherbourg
Tel: 00 33 233 93 11 23
Tariff: From FF58
Cuisine: Seafood bias
Closed: Sun

La Ciboulette
27 rue de l'Abbaye
Cherbourg
Tel: 00 33 233 93 40 41
Tariff: From FF88
Cuisine: Various + kids

Le Cavelier
9 rue du Commerce
Cherbourg
Tel: 00 33 233 53 33 27
Tariff: Various
Cuisine: Tearoom
Closed: Mon

Le Faîtout
25 rue de la Tour Carée
Cherbourg
Tel: 00 33 233 04 25 04
Tariff: Approx. FF105
Cuisine: French Bistro
Closed: Sun, Mon lunch &
two weeks over
Christmas.

Le Grandgousier
21 rue de l'Abbaye
Cherbourg
Tel: 00 33 233 53 19 43
Tariff: From FF100
Cuisine: Gastronomic fish
restaurant. Most dishes
served with a dollop of
caviar.
Closed: Sat lunchtime,
Sun pm, Mon in winter.

La Moulerie
73 rue au Blé
Cherbourg
Tel: 00 33 233 01 11 90
Tariff: From FF80
Cuisine: Mussels galore ,
served in huge bowls, with
wine-based sauces.
Closed: Sun, Mon lunch

Oncle Scott's
24-26 rue du Château
Cherbourg
Tel: 00 33 233 93 03 50
Tariff: From FF39. Children
under 5 eat free. Kids
under 12 years FF30
Cuisine: Various
Open: 12-3pm/7-midnight
Closed: Sun

Les Trois Capitaines
16 quai de Caligny
Cherbourg
Tel: 00 33 233 20 11 66
Tariff: From FF80
Cuisine: Seafood
Closed: Mon lunchtime

Le Vauban
22 quai de Caligny
Cherbourg
Tel: 00 33 233 43 10 11
Tariff: From FF90
Cuisine: French. View
over the quay.
Closed: Mon

Yacht-Club
Port de Plaisance
Cherbourg
Behind the Napoleon
statue.
Tel: 00 33 233 53 02 83
Tariff: From FF84
Cuisine: Gastonomic
French cuisine,
particulary seafood.
Panoramic view over the
marina.
Open: 12-2pm and 7-
10.30. Bar: 9.30pm-1am.

> **Specialities of
> Deauville**
>
> Seafood such as
> **moules à la crème aux
> crevettes** is very
> popular

**Restaurants of
Deauville**
Deauville's restaurants
tend to be expensive.

Augusto
27 rue Désiré Le Hoc
Deauville
Tel: 00 33 231 88 34 49
Tariff: From FF149
Cuisine: Fine French
Closed: Tues, Wed lunch
& 10 Jan-10 Feb

Aux Landiers
90 rue Louvel et Brière
Deauville
Tel: 00 33 231 88 00 39
Tariff: From FF98
Cuisine: Fine French
Closed: Wed, Thurs lunch
except July & August

Bistrot les 4 Chats
8 rue d'Orléans
Deauville
Tel: 00 33 231 88 94 94
Tariff: From FF200
Cuisine: Traditional
Closed: Wed, Thurs

Brasserie Cateliene
73 rue Désiré Le Hoc
Deauville
Tel: 00 33 231 88 36 51
Tariff: Various
Cuisine: Bar Brasserie
Closed: Wed.

Le Ciro's
Boulevard de la Mer
Deauville
Tel: 00 33 231 14 31 31
Tariff: From FF195
Cuisine: Fine Seafood
Closed: Tues eve., Wed,

Crêperie du Plaza
64 rue Mirabeau
Deauville
Tel: 00 33 231 98 91 49
Tariff: Various
Cuisine: Fast food
Closed: Wed

Il Parasole
6 rue Hoche
Deauville
Tel: 00 33 231 81 64 64
Tariff: From FF79
Cuisine: Italian
Closed: Tues, Wed lunch

Le Yearling
38 avenue Hocquart-de-Turtot
Deauville
Tel: 00 33 231 88 33 37
Tariff: From FF135
Cuisine: Norman
Closed: Mon, Tues

Specialities of Honfleur
Check out the prawns, shrimps and fois gras

Restaurants of Honfleur

L'Assiette Gourmande
2 quai des Passagers
Honfleur
Tel: 00 33 231 89 24 88
Tariff: From FF170
Cuisine: Modern French
Closed: Mon

Eating Out

L'Auberge du Vieux Clocher
9 rue de L'Homme de Bois
Honfleur
Tel: 00 33 231 89 12 06
Tariff: From FF135
Cuisine: Norman
Closed: Mon, Tues

Les Cascades
17 place Thiers
Honfleur
Tel: 00 33 231 89 05 83
Tariff: Various
Cuisine: Traditional

La Ciderie
26 place Hamelin
Honfleur
Tel: 00 33 231 89 59 85
Tariff: Various
Cuisine: Creperie
Closed: Wed.

Taverne de la Mer
35 rue Haute
Honfleur
Tel: 00 33 231 89 57 77
Tariff: From FF119
Cuisine: Fish
Closed: Mon & Tues am.

Specialities of Mont-Saint-Michel
Amazingly filling and superbly fluffy omelettes definitely have to be tasted. Lamb is also a firm favourite on the Mount.

Restaurants of Mont-Saint-Michel

Auberge Saint-Pierre
In the ramparts of Mont St Michel
Tel: 00 33 231 60 09 33
Tariff: From FF90
Cuisine: Norman. Staff where Norman costume
Closed: 15-15 Feb.

La Mère Poulard
Intra Muros, BP 18
Mont St Michel
Famous its fluffy omelettes as eaten by Leon Trotsky and Margaret Thatcher.
Tariff: From FF90
Tel: 00 33 233 60 14 03

Check-Out
The Automatic
Check-Ins

If you are looking to stay overnight or longer on a budget, then any of France's budget hotels may be a good option. For these hotels, functionality is the primary concern, so no room service, luxurious towels, beautiful furniture or scenic views.

But they are usually situated close to the motorway networks, so you can check-in and out and be back on route with ease.

These hotels operate on an unmanned auto-check-in basis. Entrance is by credit card through a 'hole in the wall' using the language of your choice, and you have 24 hour access. The rooms are clean, functional and usually comprise a double and a single bed (bunk) plus a colour TV.

The Formule 1 hotel is cheap at around £19 per night for up to 3 people but the shower and toilet is communal - most annoying if you get into the shower only to find you have forgotten the

BUDGET HOTELS IN FRANCE			
Name	Room price from FF	Beds/ room	Central Reservation
B&B	160	4	00 33 2 98 33 75 00
Bonsai	149	3	00 33 1 42 46 15 45
Formule 1	119	3	00 33 1 49 21 90 75
Mister Bed	149	4	00 33 1 46 14 38 00

soap! Worse, still if you get back to your room to find you have forgotten the entry code!

Restaurants are never part of the internal landscape of a budget hotel, but there is a snack vending machine which is always accessible. In the morning a simple Continental breakfast, though not cordon bleue, is good value for money at around £2.50 per person.

The majority of hotels are one and two star hotels and prices tend to vary depending on location and comfort. The chain hotels can generally be relied upon to deliver a good quality of service within their star rating. For instance, you can expect a TV, telephone and an en-suite shower room as part of the package in a two star hotel. A bathroom would cost more.

Chambres d'hotes are becoming popular in France. These are French style bed and breakfasts, mostly run by ordinary people who have turned their private homes into

1 & 2 STAR HOTEL CHAINS IN FRANCE	
Tariffs vary between £20-£60 per room	
Name	Central Reservation
Balladins *	00 33 1 64 62 49 99
Campanile - Motel style	00 33 1 64 62 46 46
Ibis-Arcade **	00 33 1 69 91 05 63
Logis de France * / ** / ***	00 33 1 45 84 83 84

touristic accommodation.

For accommodation with more than a dash of panache, and a huge sprinkling of French flavour, try a chateau. Châteaux make for beautiful retreats and are usually situated out of town surrounded by greenery and nature. One such hotel is the **Hotel du Vieux Château**. This authentic medieval castle, surrounded by its ramparts, in the heart of the Contentin Peninsula (22km from Cherbourg) is highly recommended. It has its own gastronomic restaurant within the old knights' hall and the accommodation has an olde worlde charm and ambience.

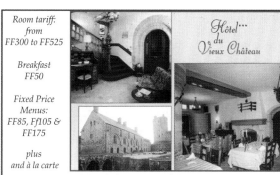

*Room tariff:
from
FF300 to FF525*

*Breakfast
FF50*

*Fixed Price
Menus:
FF85, Ff105 &
FF175*

*plus
and à la carte*

*Hôtel···
du
Vieux Château*

*Hotel du Vieux Château
4, cours du Château, 50260 Bricquebec
Tel: 02 33 52 24 49 Fax: 02 33 52 62 71
Take N13 and leave at the Bircquebec exit,
taking the D900 in the direction of Bricquebe.*

Camping is a very popular family option in France and with over 11000 farms and nature preserved camping areas to choose throughout France there must be something to suit. The official 1 to 4 star gradings are awarded by the French Federation of Camping and Caravanning Camping outside of a legal camp grounds is forbidden. However it is acceptable to camp near a farm. More information can be obtained from the guide 'Bienvenue à la Ferme Tel: 00 33 (0)1 47 23 55 40

For further information contact:

Fédération française de camping-caravanning
French Federation of Camping & Caravanning
78 rue de Rivoli, 75004 Paris
Tel: 0033 (0)1 42 72 84 08

Hotels

Hotels in Bayeux

Motel Amazone**
Boulevard Winston Churchill
Saint-Vogor-Le-Grand
Bayeux
Modern hotel between the sea
and the forest
Tariff: From FF200
Tel: 00 33 231 21 59 10

Hôtel d'Argouges
21 rie Saint Patrice
Bayeux
18th century mansion faces a
square near the town
Tariff: From FF280
Tel: 00 33 231 92 88 86

Hôtel Le Bayeux**
9 rue Tardif
Bayeux
Near Cathedral. Two rooms
equipped for handicapped
Tariff: From FF230
Tel: 00 33 231 92 70 08

Family Home
39 rue Général-Dais
Bayeux, Central guest house
Tariff: From FF150
Tel: 00 33 231 92 15 22

Le Lion d'Or***
71 rue St Jean
Bayeux
Tariff: From FF430
Tel: 00 33 231 92 06 90

Hotels in Cabourg

Auberge des Viviers **
81 avenue Charles de Gaulle
Cabourg
Near the beach and golf
course.
Tariff: From 250
Closed Jan 1 to 15 Feb
Tel: 00 33 231 91 05 10

Le Grand Hôtel****
Promenade Marcel-Proust
Cabourg
Sea Views. Makes good use
of its Proust (the author)
connections.
Tariff: From FF490. You can
hire Proust's room (room
414) for FF1200.
Tel: 00 33 235 84 21 51

L'Oie Qui Fume**
(The Smoking Goose)
18 avenue de la Brèche-
Buhot, Cabourg
Very quiet & comfortable
Tariff: From FF300
Tel: 0033 235 84 53 75
Closed 1 Jan o 15 Feb

Hôtel du Golf**
avenue de l'Hippodrome
Cabourg
In between the golf course
and the Hippodrome
Tariff: FF150
Tel: 00 33 235 84 89 98

Hotels

Hotels in Caen

Hôtel Bernieres*
50 ru du Bernières
Caen
Central, halfway between St-
Pierre & St-Jean churches
Tariff: From FF180
Tel: 00 33 231 86 01 26

Hôtel Cordeliers**
4 rue des Cordeliers
Caen
Set in own garden in small
pedestrian street near castle.
Tariff: From FF150
Tel: 00 33 231 8637 14

Hôtel Courtonne**
Place Courtonne
Caen
Overlooks pleasure port
Tariff: From FF280
Tel: 00 33 231 93 47 83

Hôtel Mercure***
rue de Courtonne, Caen
Overlooks yacht basin
Tariff: From FF460
Tel: 00 33 231 47 43 88

Holiday Inn-City Centre***
place Foch, Caen
Near Hippodrome, 10 mins.
walk from the centre
Tariff: From FF505
Tel: 00 33 231 27 57 57

Hotels in Cherbourg

Note: the nearest campsite
from the ferry terminal is
:Camping de Collignon, 3km
away towards Barfleur at
Tourlaville. You can contact
them on 00 33 233 20 16 88.

Ambassadeurs Hôtel
22 quai de Caligny
Cherbourg
Parking available and there
is a restaurant.
Tariff: From approx FF160
Tel: 00 33 233 43 10 00

Hôtel Croix de Malte**
5 rue des Halles
Cherbourg
Shabby outside, lovely inside
by the side of the theatre
Tariff: From FF160
Tel: 00 33 233 44 01 11

Hôtel Le Louvre**
2 rue Henri Dunant
Cherbourg
On semi-pedestrianised road
Tariff: From FF175
Tel: 00 33 233 175

Hôtel Mercure
Gare Maritime
Cherbourg
Near the ferry terminal
Tariff: From FF425
Tel: 00 33 233 44 01 11

Hôtel Moderna**
28 rue Marine
Cherbourg
Central location
Tariff: From FF170
Tel: 00 33 233 43 05 30

Hôtel Régence
42 quai de Caligny
Cherbourg
A pleasant Logis de France
hotel which has its own
parking facility. Faces the
harbour and has a
restaurant.
Tariff: From approx. FF280
Tel: 00 33 233 43 05 16

Hôtel de la Renaissance
4 rue de l"Eglise
Cherbourg
Located in a nice part of
town. Faces the port so
some rooms have sea views.
Tariff: From FF280
Tel: 00 33 233 43 23 90

**To Dial From France
omit 00 33
and add
0**

Hotels in Deauville

Hôtel du Golf****
Mont Canisy, St-Arnoult
Deauville
Magnificent setting on Mont
Canisy. Own golf course,
floorshow & casino
Tariff: From FF850
Tel: 00 33 231 14 24 00

Hôtel Ibis**
9-10 quai de la Marine
Deauville
Close to port, nice garden
Tariff: From FF330
Tel: 00 33 231 14 50 00

Hôtel Normandy****
38 rue Jean Mermoz
Deauville
Tariff: From FF1100
Tel: 00 33 231 98 66 22

Park Hôtel***
81 avenue de la Républic
Deauville
An ancient villa, central site.
Tariff: From FF690
Tel: 00 33 231 88 09 71

Hôtel Les Sports**
27 rue Gambetta
Deauville
Behind the fish market
Tariff: From FF300
Tel: 00 33 231 88 22 67

Hotels in Honfleur

It is difficult to find parking near a central hotel.

Le Castel Albertine***
19 cours Albert-Manuel
Honfleur
19th century manor house on the main approach road. Own parking..
Tariff: From FF400
Tel: 00 33 231 98 85 56

Auberge de la Claire**
77 cours Albert Manuel
Honfleur
Own parking.
Tariff: From FF250
Tel: 00 33 231 89 05 95

L'Ecrin***
119 rue Eugène Boudin
Honfleur
18th century town house, own courtyard, quiet - four poster beds. Own car park.
Tariff: From FF420
Tel: 00 33 231 98 85 56

Motel Monet
Cherrière du Puits
Honfleur
Functional & clean, 10 mins from town. Own parking.
Tariff: From FF250
Tel: 00 33 231 89 00 90
Closed: Throughout January

Hotels in Mont-St-Michel

Hôtel La Mère Poulard***
Intra Muros, BP 18
Mont St Michel
Famous hotel known for its fluffy omellettes as eaten by Leon Trotsky and Margaret Thatcher.
Tariff: From FF390
Tel: 00 33 233 60 14 03

Les Oiseaux De La Mer
Guest House
Le Bas-Courtils, 9km from Mont St Michel
Charming location, restored stables non-stop service
Tariff: Variable so on request
6 rooms & 3 gîtes for 5 people
Tel: 00 33 233 70 95 81

Auberge St Pierre
Grande Rue, Mont St Michel
15 century building classed as an historic monument, built into the ramparts. Great restaurant where staff are dressed in Norman costumes.
Tariff: From FF330
Tel: 00 33 233 60 14 03

Le Relais du Roy***
Route du Mont
Mont St Michel
Has a restaurant with medieval setting
Tariff: From FF350
Tel: 00 33 233 60 14 25

How Much Can You Bring Back?

In theory there are no limits on the amount of alcohol or tobacco for personal use.
In practice exceeding Advisory Guidelines means you could be stopped

Since 1st January 1993, you are permitted to bring back as much alcohol and tobacco as you like, but it must be for personal use only. So you can happily stock up for Christmas or parties or weddings.

Although H. M. Customs and Excise have no authority to limit the amount you bring back into this country they do have the right to stop you if your purchases exceed the 'Advisory Guidelines'. In this case you may be required to prove that the goods are for your own personal use.

If you are stopped, remember that the H.M. Customs officer is looking for bootleggers or those intent on resale and your co-operation will be appreciated. Other products such as mineral water, or any other non-alcoholic or food products are not limited in any way. Enjoy.

Advisory Guidelines
as set by H.M. Customs & Excise

Wine (not to exceed 60 litres of sparkling wine)	90 litres
Spirits	10 litres
Intermediate products (i.e port & sherry)	20 litres
Beer	110 litres
Cigarettes	800
Cigarillos	400
Cigars	200
Tobacco	1 Kilogram

Conversion Tables

What's Your Size?
When buying clothes in France, check the conversion tables below to find out your size:

Women's Shoes

GB		FR	GB		FR
3	=	35½	5½	=	39
3½	=	36	6	=	39½
4	=	37	6½	=	40
4½	=	37½	7	=	40½
5	=	38	8	=	41½

Women's Dresses/Suits

GB		FR	GB		FR
8	=	36	14	=	42
10	=	38	16	=	44
12	=	40	18	=	46

Women's Blouses/Sweaters

GB		FR	GB		FR
30	=	36	36	=	42
32	=	38	38	=	44
34	=	40	40	=	46

Men's Shirts

GB		FR	GB		FR
14½	=	37	16	=	41
15	=	38	16½	=	42
15½	=	39/40	17	=	43

Men's Suits

GB		FR	GB		FR
36	=	46	42	=	52
38	=	48	44	=	54
40	=	50	46	=	56

Men's Shoes

GB		FR	GB		FR
7	=	40	10	=	43
8	=	41	11	=	44
9	=	42	12	=	45
			13	=	46

Weights and Measures:

Distance 1.6 km=		1 mile
Weight 1 kg	=	2.20lbs
Liquid 4.54 litres=		1 gallon
Liquid 1 litre	=	1.76 pints
Length 1m	=	39.37inches
Area 1sq metre	=	1.196 sq yds

Speed

kpm	mph	kpm	mph
50	31	100	62
70	43	110	68
80	50	120	75
90	56	130	81

Out and About in France

*A few essential tips
to make your
travels a little easier ...*

En Route:
To comply with French motoring regulations, please note what is and is not essential:

It is essential:
* To have a full UK driving licence and all motoring documents.
* To be over the age of 18 - even if you have passed your test in the UK.
* Not to exceed 90km/h in the first year after passing your test.
* To display a GB sticker or Euro number plate
* To carry a red warning triangle.
* To wear rear seat belts if fitted.
* To affix headlamp diverters. These are widely available in motoring shops or DIY with black masking tape.

It is not essential to:
* To have a green card
* To have yellow headlights.

Parking:
Illegal parking in France can be penalised by a fine, wheel clamping or vehicle removal. Park wherever you see a white dotted line or if there are no markings at all.

There are also numerous 'pay and display' meters. (horodateurs) where small change is required to buy a ticket. The ticket should be displayed inside the car windscreen on the driver's side.

If you find a blue parking zone (zone bleue), this will be indicated by a blue line on the pavement or road and a blue signpost with a white letter P. If there is a square under the P then you have to display a cardboard disc which has various times on it. They allow up to two and a half hours parking time. The discs are available in supermarkets or petrol stations and are sometimes given away free. Ask for a **'disque de stationnement'**.

Motorways & Roads:
French motorways (autoroutes) are marked by blue and white 'A' signs. Many motorways are privately owned and outside towns a toll charge (péage) is usually payable and can be expensive. This can be paid by credit card (Visa Card, Eurocard, Mastercard), cash or even coins at automatic gates so be prepared. Contact a tourist board for the exact cost. Alternatively if you have access to the internet click on **www.autoroutes.fr.**

Roads are indicated as:

A roads -
Autoroutes - Motorways

D roads -
Routes départementales - scenic alternatives to 'A' roads.

C roads -
routes communales - country roads.

'N Roads -
routes nationales - toll free, single lane roads. Slower than 'A' roads.

Breakdown on Motorways:
If you should be unlucky enough to breakdown on the motorway and you do

---

IMPORTANT!

DRIVE ON THE RIGHT, OVERTAKE ON THE LEFT

IMPORTANT!

IF THERE ARE NO STOP SIGNS AT INTERSECTIONS, CARS MUST YIELD TO THE RIGHT

Out and About in France

not have breakdown cover, **DON'T PANIC** you can still get assistance. There are emergency telephones stationed every mile and a half on the motorway. These are directly linked to the local police station. The police are able to automatically locate you and arrange for an approved repair service to come to your aid.

Naturally there is a cost for this and fees are regulated. Expect to pay around £50 for labour plus parts and around £55 for towing.

An extra 25% supplement is also charged if you break down between 6pm and 8am and any time on Saturdays, Sundays and national holidays!

At the garage, ensure you ask for un Ordre de Réparation (repair quote) which you should sign. This specifies the exact nature of the repairs, how long it will take to repair your vehicle and, most importantly, the cost!

Emergency Phrases:

Please, help
Aidez-moi s'il vous plaît

My car has broken down
Ma voiture est en panne

I have run out of petrol
Je suis en panne d'essence

The engine is overheating
Le moteur surchauffe

There is a problem with the brakes
Il y a un problème de freins

I have a flat tyre
J'ai un pneu crevé

The battery is flat
La batterie est vide

There is a leak in the petrol tank/in the radiator
Il y a une fuite dans le réservoir d'essence/dans le radiateur

Can you send a mechanic/breakdown van?
Pouvez vous envoyer un mécanicien/une dépanneuse?

Can you tow me to a garage?
Pouvez-vous me remorquer jusqu'à un garage?

I have had an accident
J'ai eu un accident

The windscreen is shattered
Le pare-brise est cassé

Call an ambulance
Appelez une ambulance

Out and About in France

Speed Limits:
In France speed limits are shown in kilometres per hour **not** miles per hour. Always adhere to these speed limits as in France they are strictly enforced:

	MPH	km/h
Toll motorways	81	130
Dual Carriageways	69	110
Other Roads	55	90
Towns	31	50

When raining, these speed limits are reduced by 6mph on the roads and 12mph on the motorway. In fog, speed is restricted to 31mph. As well as speed traps, it is useful to know that entrance and exit times through the toll booths can be checked on your toll ticket and may be used as evidence of speeding!

Roadside Messages:
For safety's sake, it is very important to be aware of the following roadside messages:

Carrefour	Crossroad
Déviation	Diversion

Priorité à droite
Give way to traffic on the right

Péage	Toll
Vous n'avez pas la priorité	Give way
Ralentir	Slow down
Rappel	Restriction continues
Sens unique	One way
Serrez à droite/ à gauche	Keep right/ Keep left
Véhicules lents	Slow vehicles

Other messages:
Gravillons	Loose chippings
Chaussée Déformée	Uneven road & temporary surface
Nids de Poules	Potholes

Tyre Pressure:
It is crucial to ensure that your tyres are at the correct pressure to cater for heavy loads. Make sure you do not exceed the car's maximum carrying weight.

The following table gives a guide to how heavy typical loads are:

		Weight	
1 case of	Qty	kg	lbs
Wine	x 2	15kg	33lbs
Champagne	x12	22kg	48lbs
Beer 25cl	x 2	8kg	18lbs

Out and About in France

Traffic News:
Tune in to Autoroute FM107.7 for French traffic news in English and French.

Drink Driving:
UK drink/drive laws are mild at 80mg alcohol, compared to France. French law dictates that a 50g limit of alcohol is allowed - just 1 glass of wine. Exceeding this limit risks confiscation of your licence, impounding of the car, a prison sentence or an on-the- spot fine of anything between 200FF (£22) to 30,000FF (almost £3,100!)

Filling Up:
To fill up, head for petrol stations attached to the hypermarkets (i.e. Auchan, Continent, Intermarché, E. Leclerc, PG) as these offer the best value fuel. Petrol stations on the motorway - autoroutes - tend to be the most expensive. Though sterling and travellers cheques are not accepted, credit cards usually are. Some petrol stations have automated payment facilities by credit card. These are generally 24 hour petrol stations and tend to be unmanned in the evening but do not rely on them for fuel salvation as they often do not accept international credit cards!

Currently petrol is cheaper in France - diesel is much cheaper in France.

Petrol grades are as follows:

Unleaded petrol -
l'essence sans plomb. Available in 95 & 98 grades - equates to UK premium and super grades respectively.

Leaded petrol -
l'essence or Super
Graded as:
90 octane (2 star),
93 octane (3 star)
97 octane (4 star).
Gazole - Diesel Fuel
GPL - LPG (liquefied petroleum gas)

IMPORTANT!
CHILDREN UNDER 10 ARE NOT ALLOWED TO TRAVEL IN THE FRONT

Out and About in France

Caught on the Hop!
Cafés generally allow you to use their toilets for free. In shopping complexes you may require a 1FF coin to gain entry. If you see a white saucer, place a coin or two in it. In the streets you may come across the Sanisette, a white cylindrical shaped building. Insert 2FF in the slot to open the door. After use the Sanisette completely scrubs and polishes itself.

Shopping by Credit Card:
To use your credit card ensure that you have your passport handy as you may be expected to produce it.

Shopping:
Supermarket trolleys (les chariots) require a (refundable) 10 franc piece. Keep one handy to avoid queuing for change.

Shopping Hours:
Shops and supermarkets open and close as follows:

Open	9.00 am
Close lunch-time	12.00 noon
Open again	2.00 pm
Close finally	5.00-7.00 pm

Most shops are closed on Sunday and some on Monday.

Public Holidays:
Most French shops will be shut on the following days

Jan 1	New Year	Jour de l'an
Apr*	Easter Monday	Lundi de Pâques
May 1	Labour Day	Fête du Travail
May 8	Victory Day	Armistice1945
May*	Ascension	Ascension
May*	Whitsun	Lundi de Pentecôte
July 14	Bastille Day	Fête nationale
Aug 15	Assumption	Assomption
Nov 1	All Saints'	Toussaint
Nov 11	Armistice Day	Armistice 1918
Dec 25	Christmas	Noël
*Dates change each year.		

Tipping:
Tipping is widely accepted in France. However restaurant menus with the words 'servis compris' indicate that service is included but small change can be left if so desired. The following is the accepted norm for tipping:

Restaurants service usually included	Optional
Cafés service usually included	Optional
Hotels	No
Hairdressers	10F
Taxis	10F
Porters	10F
Cloakroom attendants	Small change
Toilets	Small change

Out and About in France

Phoning Home:
Phonecards (Télécartes) are widely used and available at travel centres, post offices, tobacconists and shops displaying the Télécarte sign. Coin operated payphones (becoming rare) take 1,2 & 5 FF coins. Cheap rate (50% extra time) is between 22.30hrs-08.00hrs Monday to Friday, 14.00hrs-08.00hrs Saturday, all day Sunday & public holidays.
To call the UK dial 00, at the dialling tone dial 44 followed by the phone number and omit 0 from the STD code.

Writing Home:
Post Offices (PTT) are open Monday to Friday during office hours and half day on Saturday. Smaller branches tend to close between noon and 2pm. Stamps can also be purchased from tobacconists. The cost of a postcard home is FF2.80. The small but bright yellow post boxes are easy to spot

Taxi!
It is cheaper to hail a taxi in the street or look for cab ranks indicated by the letter 'T' rather than order one by telephone. This is because a telephone requested taxi will charge for the time taken to reach you. Taxi charges are regulated. The meter must show the minimum rate on departure and the total amount (tax included) on arrival. If the taxi driver agrees that you share the taxi ride, he has the right to turn the meter back to zero at each stop showing the minimum charge again.

A tip *(pourboire)* is expected. It is customary to pay 10-15%.

No Smoking!
The French have an etiquette for everything and that includes smoking. It is forbidden to smoke in public places. However, there are quite often spaces reserved in cafés and restaurants for smokers.

Out and About in France

Money Matters:

Currency:
French currency, known as the French Franc is shown in 3 ways: FF, Fr or F. A Franc is roughly equivalent to 11p.

The French Franc is made up of 100 centimes.

Centimes have their own set of coins *(pièces)* i.e. 5, 10, 20 and 50 centimes - marked as 1/2F.

Francs are in 1, 2, 5, 10 and 20F pieces and bank notes *(billets)* are in 20, 50, 100, 200 and 500F notes.

When you are looking at a price tag, menu or receive a receipt be aware that unlike the British system of separating pounds and pence with a decimal point, in France there is no decimal point, the francs and centimes are separated by a comma

Unlimited currency may be taken into France but you must declare bank notes of 50,000 French Francs or more if your are bringing this back.

Note: The Euro became legal currency in France on January 1 1999. All prices are displayed in French Francs and Euros. The Franc will be phased out on 30 June 2002.

Currency Exchange:
Changing money from Sterling to French Francs tends to be expensive. We recommend that you use your credit card to pay for goods abroad, as credit card companies give a better rate of exchange and do not charge currency commission when buying goods abroad.

Of course you will require some cash. Change your money in the UK where it can be a little more competitive than in France.

In France you can also change money and cash travellers cheques at the Post Office (PTT), banks, stations and private bureaux de change.

Out and About in France

In hypermarket complexes there are machines available to change your Sterling to French Francs. AVOID these as they are the most expensive method for changing money. It would be better to make a purchase in the hypermarket in Sterling, as change is given in French Francs without commission charges. Although this is convenient, always be aware of the exchange rate. Some shops do take advantage.

French Franc travellers cheques can be used as cash and if you wish to turn them into cash at a French bank you will receive the face value - no commission. **Most banks in France do not accept Eurocheques any more.**

Credit Cards:
If you do choose to pay by credit card and your card has been rejected in a shop or restaurant, it could be that their card reading machine does not recognise it - some French credit cards have a 'puce', a microchip with security information on it. British cards do not have this. In this event, French tourist authorities recommend you say:

"les cartes anglaises ne sont pas des cartes â puce, mais â band magnétique. Ma carte est valable et je vous serais reconnsaissant d'en demander la confirmation auprès de votre banque ou de votre centre de traitement.'

which means
'English cards don't have an information chip, but a magnetic band. My card is valid and I would be grateful if you would confirm this with your bank or processing centre.'

If you need to contact
Barclaycard
Tel: 01604 234234
Visa
Tel: 01383 621166
Visa in France
Tel: 01 45 67 84 84

Out and About in France

Cashpoints

You can use your cashpoint card to get local currency from French cash-dispensing machines. This service is available at major banks such as:

Crédit Lyonnais,
Crédit Agricole
Crédit Mutuel

If the machine bears the same logo as that displayed on your card, such as Visa or Delta, then you can insert your card and follow the instructions. These are likely to be in English as your card will be recognised as British. Punch in your PIN and press the button marked **Envoi.** When prompted tell the machine how much you want in French Francs.

You will see phrases such as:

Tapez votre code secret - Enter your pin
Veuillez patienter - Please wait
Opération en cours - Money on its way!

Pharmacie

These are recognised by their green cross sign. The staff tend to be highly qualified so are able to give medical advice, provide first aid, and can even prescribe a range of drugs. Some drugs though are only available via a doctor's prescription (ordonnance).

Doctor

Any pharmacie will have an address of a doctor. Consultation fees are generally about £15.00. Ask for a Feuille de Soins (Statement of Treatment) if you are insured.

Medical Aid

As members of the EU, the British can get urgent medical treatment in France at reduced costs on production of a qualifying form - form E111. The E111 is available from the Department of Heath and Social Security. A refund can then be obtained in person or by post from the local Social Security Offices (Caisse Primaire d'Assurance Maladie).

Out and About in France

Passports:
Before travelling to France ensure you have a full 10 year British passport. If you are not a British National you will also require a visa and regulations vary according to your nationality. Contact the French Consulate.

Pet Passports:
Since 28 February 2000, a pilot scheme has been in force enabling cats and dogs to travel abroad without being subjected to 6 months quarantine. A blood test is required and a microchip fitted. Not more than 48 hours before return the animal must be treated for ticks and tapeworms. Only then will it be awarded the official 'pet passport'. Further information is available from PETS helpline on 0870 2411 710 or www.maf.gov.uk/animalh/quarantine.

What's The Time?
French summer starts on the last Sunday in March at 2am and ends on the last Sunday in October at 3am. Time is based on Central European Time (Greenwich Mean Time + 1 hour in winter and + 2 hours in Summer) is followed in France. This means that most of the time France is one hour ahead. The clocks are put forward 1 hour in the spring and put back 1 hour in the autumn.

Electricity:
If you wish to use any electrical appliances from the UK, you will need a Continental adaptor plug (with round pins). The voltage in France is 220V similar to 240V in the UK.

Television & Video Tapes
Another important difference is that the French standard TV broadcast system is SECAM whereas in the UK it is PAL. Ordinary video cassettes bought in France will show only in black and white. This means that French video tapes cannot be played on British videos. Be sure to ask for the VHS PAL system.

Channel Shoppers' Drinks Tips

Tips:

More expensive wines attract higher percentages of profit leaving little room for savings - if any!

A good benchmark for a maximum spend on a bottle of wine is £10.00.

If you wish to buy wines costing more than £10.00 then the UK retailers are a better bet. This is because prices at this level are comparable and it the wine is faulty it is easier to return.

The exception is Champagne which is expensive in the UK.

The price for a bottle of wine starting life at £1.00, is made up as follows:

Cost of wine	£1.00
Duty & VAT	£1.62
Shipping	£0.17
Retailer's Profit 30%	£0.78
Total cost	£3.57

Incidentally:

UK VAT is	17.5%
French VAT is	19.6%

The big cost difference is in the duty:

UK duty on a bottle of Champagne	£1.60
UK duty on a bottle of sherry	£1.40
UK duty on a bottle of still wine	£1.44
French duty on the above products	£0.04

Incidentally:

A discrepancy:
A bottle of gin bought in the UK is 37.5% proof
In France it is 47.5% proof.

The reason:
A tax avoidance tactic by the producers. If gin sold in the UK had 47.5% proof the tax on a 70cl bottle would be £6.50 instead of £5.13. A saving of £1.37.

Your Say

Guides in the Channel Hopper's Series:

Calais & Boulogne	£5.99
Dieppe, Rouen & Le Havre	£5.99
Lille	£5.99
Lower Normandy	£5.99

Special offer:
Buy two or more guides and receive
£1.00 off each guide

How to order:

- Cheques should be sent to the above address in
  favour of 'Passport Guide Publications'.
- Telephone orders welcome: 020 8905 4851
- Order on the net: **www.channelhoppers.net.**

   All guides are available at major book shops

Quick Currency Converter

FF	£@ 9.00	£@ 9.50	£@ 10.50	FF	£@ 9.00	£@ 9.50	£@ 10.50	FF	£@ 9.00	£@ 9.50	£@ 10.50
1	0.11	0.11	0.09	49	5.44	5.15	4.66	97	10.77	10.21	9.23
2	0.22	0.21	0.19	50	5.55	5.26	4.76	98	10.88	10.31	9.33
3	0.33	0.31	0.28	51	5.66	5.36	4.85	99	11.00	10.42	9.42
4	0.44	0.42	0.38	52	5.77	5.47	4.95	100	11.11	10.52	9.52
5	0.55	0.52	0.47	53	5.88	5.57	5.04	101	11.22	10.63	9.61
6	0.66	0.63	0.57	54	6.00	5.68	5.14	102	11.33	10.73	9.71
7	0.77	0.73	066	55	6.11	5.78	5.23	103	11.44	10.84	9.80
8	0.88	0.84	0.76	56	6.22	5.89	5.33	104	11.55	10.94	9.90
9	1.00	0.97	0.85	57	6.33	6.00	5.42	105	11.66	11.05	10.00
10	1.11	1.05	0.95	58	6.44	6.10	5.52	106	11.77	11.15	10.09
11	1.22	1.15	1.04	59	6.55	6.21	5.61	107	11.88	11.26	10.19
12	1.33	1.26	1.14	60	6.66	6.31	5.71	108	12.00	11.36	10.28
13	1.44	1.36	1.23	61	6.77	6.42	5.80	109	12.11	11.47	10.38
14	1.55	1.47	1.33	62	6.88	6.52	5.90	110	12.22	11.57	10.47
15	1.66	1.57	1.42	63	6.00	6.63	6.00	111	12.33	11.68	10.57
16	1.77	1.68	1.52	64	7.11	6.73	6.09	112	12.44	11.78	10.66
17	1.88	1.78	1.61	65	7.22	6.84	6.19	113	12.55	11.89	10.76
18	2.00	1.89	1.71	66	7.33	6.94	6.28	114	12.66	12.00	10.85
19	2.11	2.00	1.80	67	7.44	7.05	6.38	115	12.77	12.10	10.95
20	2.22	2.10	1.90	68	7.55	7.15	6.47	116	12.88	12.21	11.04
21	2.33	2.21	2.00	69	7.66	7.26	6.57	117	13.00	12.31	11.14
22	2.44	2.31	2.09	70	7.77	7.36	6.66	118	13.11	12.42	11.23
23	2.55	2.42	2.19	71	7.88	7.47	6.76	119	13.22	12.52	11.38
24	2.66	2.52	2.28	72	8.00	7.57	6.85	120	13.33	12.63	11.42
25	2.77	2.63	2.38	73	8.11	7.68	6.95	121	13.44	12.73	11.52
26	2.88	2.73	2.47	74	8.22	7.78	7.04	122	13.55	12.84	11.61
27	3.00	2.84	2.57	75	8.33	7.89	7.14	123	13.66	12.94	11.71
28	3.11	2.94	2.66	76	8.44	8.00	7.23	124	13.77	13.05	11.80
29	3.22	3.05	2.76	77	8.55	8.10	7.33	125	13.88	13.15	11.90
30	3.33	3.15	2.85	78	8.66	8.21	7.42	126	14.00	13.26	12.00
31	3.44	3.26	2.95	79	8.77	8.31	7.52	127	14.11	13.36	12.09
32	3.55	3.36	3.04	80	8.88	8.42	7.61	128	14.22	13.47	12.19
33	3.66	3.47	3.14	81	9.00	8.52	7.50	129	14.33	13.57	12.28
34	3.77	3.57	3.23	82	9.11	8.63	7.80	130	14.44	13.68	12.38
35	3.88	3.68	333	83	9.22	8.73	7.90	131	14.55	13.78	12.47
36	4.00	3.78	3.42	84	9.33	8.84	8.00	132	14.66	13.89	12.57
37	4.11	3.89	3.52	85	9.44	8.94	8.09	133	14.77	14.00	12.66
38	4.22	4.00	3.61	86	9.55	9.05	8.19	134	14.88	14.10	12.76
39	4.33	4.10	3.71	87	9.66	9.15	8.28	135	15.00	14.21	12.85
40	4.44	4.21	3.80	88	9.77	9.26	8.38	136	15.11	14.31	12.95
41	4.55	4.31	3.90	89	9.88	9.36	8.47	137	15.22	14.42	13.04
42	4.66	4.42	4.00	90	10.00	9.47	8.57	138	15.33	14.52	13.14
43	4.77	4.52	4.09	91	10.11	9.57	8.66	139	15.44	14.63	13.23
44	4.88	4.63	4.19	92	10.22	9.68	8.76	140	15.55	14.73	13.33
45	5.00	4.73	4.28	93	10.22	9.68	8.85	145	16.11	15.26	13.80
46	5.11	4.84	4.38	94	10.44	9.89	8.95	150	16.66	15.78	14.28
47	5.22	4.94	4.47	95	10.55	10.00	9.04	175	19.44	18.42	16.66
48	5.33	5.05	4.57	96	10.66	10.10	9.14	200	22.22	21.05	19.04